Vision Critical Studies

General Editor: Michael Egan

Henry James:
The Ibsen Years

Vision Critical Studies in preparation:

E. E. Cummings
George Gissing
D. H. Lawrence
Wyndham Lewis

HENRY JAMES:
THE IBSEN YEARS

Michael Egan

Lecturer in English,
The University of Lancaster

BOOKS
10 East 53d St., New York 10022
(a division of Harper & Row Publishers, inc.)

DALE H. GRAMLEY LIBRARY
SALEM COLLEGE
WINSTON-SALEM, N. C.

Barnes & Noble Books
Harper & Row, Publishers, Inc.
10 East 53rd Street
New York

ISBN 06-491910-2

First published in the United States 1972
© 1972 Vision Press, London

Printed and bound in Great Britain
MCMLXXII

Contents

Editorial Note

Vision Critical Studies will examine mainly nineteenth century and contemporary imaginative writing, delimiting an area of literary inquiry between, on the one hand, the loose generalities of the "reader's guide" approach and, on the other, the excessively particular specialist study. Crisply written and with an emphasis on fresh insights, the series will gather its coherence and direction from a broad congruity of approach on the part of its contributors. Each volume, based on sound scholarship and research, but relatively free from cumbersome scholarly apparatus, will be of interest and value to all students of the period.

Prefatory Note

Except where otherwise specified, all references to James's novels and tales are to first editions. The Ibsen texts used are the English translations prepared and edited for Walter Scott Ltd by William Archer. James was of course unable to read Norwegian (although he once made a brief attempt to master the language) and so far as I have been able to ascertain these were the translations he used. Unfortunately the library at Lamb House, Rye, was destroyed during World War I and of the dozen or so volumes which remain none has any connection with Ibsen or Scandinavian literature.

I would like to take this opportunity of acknowledging the great help of Professor Graham Hough and Dr John Northam, both of Cambridge University, who read the manuscript in its early form and made invaluable suggestions. Professor Philip C. McGuire of Michigan State University read the final draft with great care and I am deeply in his debt.

M.E.E.
October, 1971.

I've never quite known where our set begins and ends, and have had to content myself on this score with the indication once given me by a lady next to whom I was placed at dinner: "Oh, it's bounded on the North by Ibsen and on the South by Sargent!"

The Beldonald Holbein

Introduction

When Henry James was completing the New York edition of his *Collected Works* in 1907 he wrote somewhat wryly in a letter that the experience uncomfortably reminded him of Ozymandias— "Look on my works ye mighty!" He is indeed the most defiant of novelists: the sheer weight of his *oeuvre*, of each novel, couched in the deformed syntax of his unyielding prose, challenges both intellect and critical judgment. He dares us; he defies us; he comes within an ace of telling us to like him or lump him. In 1905 he almost said as much to his brother William who had begged him to abandon his "method of narration by interminable elaboration of suggestive reference", and, "just to please Brother", to "sit down and write a new book, with no twilight or mustiness in the plot, with great vigor and decisiveness in the action, no fencing in the dialogue, no psychological commentaries, and absolute straightness in the style." Henry retorted:

> I mean (in response to what you write me of your having read the *Golden B.*) to try to produce some uncanny form of thing, in fiction, that will gratify you, as Brother—but let me say, dear William, that I shall be greatly humiliated if you *do* like it, and thereby lump it, in your affection, with things, of the current age, that I have heard you express admiration for and that I would sooner descend to a dishonoured grave than have written. Still I *will* write you your book, on that two-and-two-make-four system on which all the awful truck that surrounds us is produced, and *then* descend to my dishonoured grave . . .

Most of James's readers, confronting the vast monument of his narrative prose fiction for the first or even second time, have despaired and moved on; like Arnold Bennett, who abandoned *The Ambassadors* after 150 pages, they find his novels "not *quite*

13

worth the great trouble" which they demand. Two apparently insurmountable difficulties bar the way. Primarily, of course, there is the question of style, that is, the felt presence of the author in any particular work. James himself was aware of this complication, but dismissed it with the remark that as soon as a writer evolves a distinctive manner it is condemned as oppressive. Again that characteristically defiant note: James was prepared to concede nothing to his public. Nevertheless the difficulty must be met, for among the most frequently voiced complaints against his work is precisely the density of his prose, and in particular the convoluted, oppressively abstract and perversely Byzantine sequence of verbal forms and ideas which he deployed during his final period. During these years—the period in which he completed the three novels of what the late F. O. Mattheissen called his "major phase"—*The Wings of the Dove* (1902), *The Ambassadors* (1903) and *The Golden Bowl* (1904)—James evolved a form of language so intensely personal, so complex and yet so defiantly abstract that to speak of its rotund oral pomposity, sententious oracular tone and infinitely discriminated parentheses, is only to begin to grapple with it.

Some readers have found it a permanent barrier to a sympathetic encounter with the James of this period. F. R. Leavis, for example, who of course places the early James in the front rank of English novelists and among those who constitute fiction's great tradition, condemns the thick, obscuring verbiage of the later manner as a symptom of Jamesian decline. "Now it is certainly true", he writes in *The Great Tradition*, "that James's development was towards over-subtlety, and that with this development we must associate a loss of sureness in his moral touch, an unsatisfactoriness that in some of the more ambitious later works leads us to question his implicit valuations." How characteristically, and how deftly, Leavis shifts his ground from a critique of style to a critique of value: James turns away from Life (that mysterious, capitalised abstraction which Leavis finds in all great writing) and thus becomes bogged down in language. Leavis's charge is a serious one, and we shall have to come back to it for it has never been adequately answered. I mention it now, however, as an example of the difficulties which James's later manner creates; and it is hardly surprising, therefore, if readers less warmly disposed towards James than Leavis turn away from his work with gestures of impatience.

The second major difficulty confronting us is what we might call the problem of perspective. Whatever our view of James's evolution—whether we see it, as Leavis does, as a parabolic curve with a peak about 1880–1886 (crowned, as it were, by *The Portrait of a Lady* and *The Bostonians*) or whether we view it more conventionally with critics like Mattheissen as a straight-line graph ascending to a climax in the major phase—it is important to grasp that with James one is dealing with a whole series of novelists rather than with a single author. Of course, varieties of style and manner, frequently sharply divergent, are to be found in almost every writer of serious pretensions; but in the case of James the characteristic is so radically pronounced, so consciously culti-vated, that, but for the author's signature, one would be hard put to recognise works from contrasting periods as issuing from the same hand.

Let me juxtapose just two passages by way of illustration. The first is from *The American*, an early novel published in 1877 when James was thirty-four. The second is from *The Golden Bowl*, one of James's last completed fictions and distanced from *The American* by nearly thirty years. What strikes one right away, however, is that the distance travelled is greater than the time; the divergences between the passages represent not only a development of style but a fundamental shift in sensibility and aesthetic which transforms not the subject matter, which is quite close, but language, point of view and stance. James's entire aesthetic meta-phor has changed.

On a brilliant day in May, in the year 1868, a gentleman was reclining at his ease on the great circular divan which at that period occupied the centre of the Salon Carré, in the Museum of the Louvre. This commodious ottoman has since been removed, to the extreme regret of all weak-kneed lovers of the fine arts; but the gentleman in question had taken serene possession of its softest spot, and, with his head thrown back and his legs outstretched, was staring at Murillo's beautiful moon-borne Madonna in profound enjoyment of his posture. He had removed his hat, and flung down beside him a little red guide-book and an opera-glass. The day was warm; he was heated with walking, and he repeatedly passed his handkerchief over his forehead, with a somewhat wearied gesture. And yet he was evidently not a man to whom fatigue was familiar; long, lean and muscular, he suggested the sort of vigour that is commonly known as "toughness." *The American*, Chapter 1

It was not until many days had passed that the Princess began to accept the idea of having done, a little, something that she was not always doing, or indeed that of having listened to any inward voice that spoke in a new tone. Yet these instinctive postponements of reflection were the fruit, positively, of recognitions and perceptions already active; of the sense, above all, that she had made, at a particular hour, made by the mere touch of her hand, a difference in the situation so long present to her as practically unattackable. This situation had been occupying, for months and months, the very centre of the garden of her life, but it had reared itself there like some strange tall tower of ivory, or perhaps rather some wonderful, beautiful but outlandish pagoda, a structure plated with hard, bright porcelain, coloured and figured and adorned, at the overhanging eaves, with silver bells that tinkled, ever so charmingly, when stirred by chance airs. She had walked round and round it—that was what she felt; she had carried on her existence in the space left her for circulation, a space that sometimes seemed ample and sometimes narrow; looking up, all the while, at the fair structure that spread itself so amply and rose so high, but never quite making out as yet where she might have entered had she wished . . . *The Golden Bowl*, Part Fourth

James continues to elaborate, in extraordinary detail, the mysterious pagoda at the centre of Maggie Verver's world. She taps it; it becomes a mosque; it may even be inhabited. The fictive shift from the first passage and its concrete detail could not be more marked.

Yet even more remarkable (simply because the manner obscures them so completely) are the similarities between the two passages. Each of these introductory sequences deploys a single American figure in relation to a European context which, as it is developed, reveals increasingly sinister overtones. The fundamental contrasts and their moral connotations in either novel—frankness opposed to deviousness, wealth to poverty, innocence to experience, even West to East—the basic contrasts of America and Europe—remain fixed over thirty years. What has changed, however, is the implicit Jamesian metaphor.

In the first passage the perspiring central figure, enjoying his ease more than the Murillo, is solitary, seated and static; his posture and locality, precisely noted in time and angle, are deliberately filled-in with graphic detail and sensuous images. The figure itself is placed squarely in the middle of the foreground, its pose held like one of the portraits hanging on the walls. In fact, the portrait metaphor is exact; James at this period consciously strove to render his sequences as complete visual units. The tough, lean American is caught in his muscular balance and Gallic context: slightly off-guard but by no means vulnerable. He is fixed in this pose sharply in our minds.

The passage from *The Golden Bowl*, however, diverges markedly from this in terms of movement, language and structure. Instead of graphic, static, visual detail, like the little red Baedecker, we are presented with a shifting, shimmering, almost floating sequence of abstractions and emotions; a scene mistily presented and the whole contained in a language both stubbornly opaque and elusively abstract. The Princess wafts in a surreal void, a strange garden where ivory towers turn into mysterious pulsating pagodas, into mosques, now cramped, now spacious, at once solid and hollow, deserted and (perhaps) inhabited. We are given not a single detail of her physical world; instead James pursues with Homeric glee his extraordinary metaphor. And his language, indulgent, luxurious, seems to rejoice almost with perversity in copulatives, intransitive verbs, negatives and the passive voice. James's prose has not simply evolved; it has undergone a complete transformation.

The shift from *The American* to *The Golden Bowl*, then, is not simply from the indicative to the passive, the concrete to the intangible. What has occurred is that the locus of attention has moved from ourselves "out there" looking down upon the portrait of a gentleman, to ourselves within the consciousness of the central figure itself, so that we are looking inwards and outwards at Europe, at the entire world east of Boston, through another mind. But the process is even more complex than this. For if we are looking outwards exclusively through the Princess's interposing vision, where are we to locate the narrative Jamesian voice which addresses us directly in the first person in the next paragraph? "If this image, however, may represent our young woman's consciousness of a recent change in her life—a change now but a few days old—it

17

must at the same time be observed that she both sought and found in renewed circulation, as I have called it, a measure of relief from the idea of having perhaps to answer for what she had done." Whose is the identity of the speaking "I"? And who is thus addressed? What James erects, as Ian Watt has argued, is a multi-dimensional quality in the narrative with the continual implication of a community of three minds—Maggie's, the narrator's, and the reader's. The action is located in a mental rather than in a (as was the case in *The American*) physical continuum. *The American* is fixed upon its canvas; *The Golden Bowl* floats freely between narrator, spectator and actor.

It seems clear, then, that as readers we should not judge the novels of the major phase in terms of the aesthetic conventions of James's apprenticeship; and further, that we should try to understand and account for the transformation which took place.

James was of course an American, born in New York in 1843. Time and place are important: James admitted himself to what he called the "complex fate" of being an American at this period and the superstitious over-evaluation of Europe (felt by so many of his early central figures) to which this gave rise. As a child he toured the Continent many times with his family, but the crucial visit occurred in 1869 when, at the age of 26, he went to Italy for the first time. Here is an extract from a letter he wrote to William about Rome:

> From midday to dusk I have been roaming the streets. Que vous en dirai-je? At last—for the first time—I live! It beats everything; it leaves the Rome of your fancy—your education—nowhere. It makes Venice—Florence—Oxford—London—seem like cities of pasteboard. I went reeling and moaning thro' the streets, in a fever of enjoyment. In the course of four or five hours I traversed almost the whole of Rome and got a glimpse of everything, the Forum, the Coliseum (stupendissimo!) the Pantheon, the Capitol, St Peter's, the column of Trajan, the castle of St Angelo—all the piazzas and ruins and monuments. The effect is something indescribable.

It is interesting and important to note the terms of James's praise—"At last for the first time I live!" In Rome, in Italy, overwhelmed by the spirit of the high Renaissance, the young James believes he has encountered "real life" for the first time. Florence, London, Oxford seem suddenly like toy cities by comparison;

Rome alone is real. But above all it is the Renaissance and Imperial Rome, as expressed through its ruins, churches and monuments which captivate. And it is here that the crucial identification of Europe with the Renaissance occurs. This is the primary point to grasp about James's attitude to Europe: it is the Europe, the Italy, the Rome of the high Renaissance which presents itself before his eyes. James articulates it in his story "Four Meetings" (1879):

> A few minutes later she put it to me: "And which country do you prefer?"
> "There's one I love beyond any. I think you'd do the same."
> Her gaze rested as on a dim revelation and then she breathed "Italy?"
> "Italy," I answered softly too; and for a moment we communed over it. She looked as pretty as if instead of showing her photographs I had been making love to her. To increase the resemblance she turned off blushing. It made a pause which she broke at last by saying: "That's the place which—in particular—I thought of going to."
> "Oh that's the place—that's the place!" I laughed.

For the next ten or twelve years in his creative life it was this conscious fusion, this deliberate confusion of the Italian Renaissance with the idea of Europe, which was to dominate his work. In *Roderick Hudson, The American* and *The Portrait of a Lady,* in almost all the early tales, the overriding presence is Europe, that is, Italy; a Europe contrasted ambiguously with America— sometimes as a force for moral good, sometimes as the embodiment of corruption—but overwhelmingly the Europe of Renaissance values.

In order to fully understand the impact of Europe on James's developing aesthetic it is important to grasp two things. The first we have already discussed: James was a mid-nineteenth century American. But—and this is the second point—he was an American novelist who aspired to write realistically about his contemporary world: that is, who aspired to produce, with an American emphasis, fictions comparable in scope and form with those of Flaubert or George Eliot. This may seem a common enough ambition; yet it is simply a fact of American literary history that, for a variety of reasons which we will look at presently, no American writer before James had succeeded in, or even attempted, such a venture. *Huckle-*

berry Finn did not appear until 1882, while the novels of Cooper, Hawthorne and Melville, whatever their considerable literary merit, had retreated from the bleak social milieu of nineteenth-century New England into varieties of allegory or romance. Thus it was James, in his early prose fictions, as Alfred Kazin remarks, who first established that emphasis on contemporary social fact which (already in full bloom in Europe) was to become the major expression of American narrative literature later in the century.

By rejecting the ethos of Hawthorne and attempting to re-define the American novel in terms of the European Realist movement James was not reacting idiosyncratically but was, along with his contemporaries, responding to the pressures of his time. As W. D. Howells wrote to T. S. Perry in 1886: "No one invented realism; rather it seems to have come spontaneously all at once and everywhere."

Howells's remark reveals the readiness with which he and his friends, including James, responded to the new movement as soon as they encountered it. Realism, which had its origins in France and England during the mid-1850s, was a stylistic ideology whose terms are inseparable from the values and ambitions of the bourgeois society which created it. This point needs some stressing because realism, as a term of literary description—usually taken to denote the presence of convincing, unidealised personal detail such as dirty hair or disjointed forms of speech—has gradually become confused with the nineteenth-century aesthetic which so impressed Henry James. Yet as Erich Auerbach overwhelmingly argued in *Mimesis*, the inclusion of this kind of unidealised detail can be found in the work of almost every major writer in the history of literature, from Homer through Euripides, the Elizabethans and to the present. Realism, in Auerbach's sense, is a notion relative to the decisive class in the economy; or, as Alfred Kazin put it, attachment to the real is always the mark of a class in the ascendant. When Aristotle advised tragedians to ensure that their kings behaved in a kingly fashion, and to see that their slaves behaved slavishly, he was implicitly articulating the same truth. Realism, in the relative sense, is the serious, heroic and even tragic treatment, in art, of the ruling class.

This notion was only partially perceived by the nineteenth-century Realists. Their demands, never clearly articulated, incidentally, appeared to be purely aesthetic. Art was to be wholly objective. Its function was to catalogue, with scientific detachment, contemporary social fact. The artist was not to moralise; nor was he to judge. Any subject, as long as it was dealt with rigorously, was as good as any other—Yvetot, in Flaubert's famous remark, was worth as much as Constantinople. Yet behind each of these positives stood a negative: the refusal to moralise because nothing is absolute; the refusal to idealise because life is harsh; the rejection of Romanticism because it is an evasion of the real. What this negativism cloaked in its turn, however, was the half-perceived truth that literary forms, in the modern, nineteenth-century world, had failed to keep pace with the evolving social milieu. The demand that writing should again be made "real" implicitly recognised that since the end of the Napoleonic wars at least literature had failed to shed its feudal trappings. Writers continued to work within the old conventions, the old realism, and thus laid themselves open to the charge that they were being "unreal"—that is to say, that they were dealing with a spectrum of values and assumptions, with a world, which bore no relation to the contemporary. Thus "Realism", as a literary movement, was in practise the banner under which the European middle classes, who reached the height of their social influence and economic power in the latter half of the nineteenth century, demanded that they be treated both heroically and seriously, even tragically, in literature. In their rejection of traditional forms the Realist writers in fact were attempting to establish a vehicle within which it would be possible, for the first time, to define the emergent bourgeoisie. Their demands, although presented as an aesthetic manifesto, were closely identified with the ideological needs of the new ruling class.

Of course Henry James, born into the Boston bourgeoisie and educated largely in Europe, identified himself with the new movement almost as soon as he encountered it. He perceived accurately and immediately that in the United States there simply was no established middle class, with all its self-confident social codes and forms, comparable with that to be found in Europe. In his short study of Hawthorne, published in 1879, he expressed himself precisely in these terms, cataloguing in some famous passages all those middle class institutions (and the social forms and usages they implied) which America lacked and England possessed—Eton, Ascot, Epsom and all the rest of it. So if I can draw together all the points I've made so far, we can say that by his attachment to realism James aspired to portray accurately in fiction contemporary middle class society; but it was only in Europe, a Europe which he clothed in the mystique of the Italian Renaissance, that he was able to find the kind of social context in which to work. His decision was therefore to emigrate and settle over here.

It should now be clearer why the metaphor of the portrait was so important for the early James. He wished to catch his contemporary world in a characteristic pose, fix it in all its bourgeois detail for posterity. With his love for the achievement of the Renaissance—his aspiration to achieve in fiction something as artistically powerful—the metaphor was ready to hand. *The Portrait of a Lady*—the very title evokes the ethos of the Ufizzi—was the crowning consequence of this period. All of his work of this time is a succession of portraits, partial or otherwise, of ladies and gentlemen, usually Americans, in search of something Europe is unable to give them.

After about 1890, however, the Jamesian metaphor undergoes severe moderation. His goals remained the same: the faithful representation of contemporary reality within a literary frame. But, with only one or two exceptions, his novels were being received with an almost universal lack of enthusiasm. Everyone acknowledged that he was a great writer; no one bothered to read him. Worse still, hardly any one bought his books. "My books don't sell and it looks as though my plays might", he wrote to Robert Louis Stevenson in 1891. He had decided to become a playwright.

I don't want to give the impression, however, that James turned to the theatre exclusively or even primarily out of monetary need. The plea of poverty cloaked his excitement; it is clear from his letters and notebooks that he gloried in the artistic challenge which the theatrical form offered. Here was an alternative to painting portraits. True, he continued to think of the proscenium arch as framing the action; but the stage provided him with an accessible formula for integrating and relating his series of canvasses. He threw himself with relish into dramatising *The American* for the Compton Comedy Company in 1889.

The story of James's troubled five years at the box-office, from 1890 to 1895, has been well told and documented. Most of the relevant papers, together with the texts, are to be found in Leon Edel's edition of the plays (Rupert Hart-Davis, 1949). What we should note here, however, is that in 1895 James's theatrical adventure came to a disastrous conclusion. He had staked everything, a final throw as it were, upon one last play, *Guy Domville*, the story of a Catholic priest who is caught between the demands of his religious vocation and the call of the world. Unfortunately the first night was wholly calamitous and concluded with James being booed from the stage. The evening began to disintegrate during the second act with an absurd drinking scene, subsequently deleted; and it fell apart completely when the leading lady was greeted with a chorus of "Where did you get that hat?" as she entered wearing an extravagant *chapeau*. By the end of the evening the house was virtually in chaos. Defeat became a rout when, in response to Guy's concluding words, "I am the last, my lord, of the Domvilles", someone called out, "It's a bloody good thing you are!" George Alexander, the leading man, withdrew white-faced and miserable. As H. G. Wells later recalled: "By nature Alexander had a long face, but at that moment, with audible defeat before him, he seemed the longest and dismallest face, all face, that I have even seen. The slowly-closing door reduced him to a strip, a line, of perpendicular gloom."

As the curtain came down and the actors were being politely if coldly applauded, James arrived at the stage door. Half-aware of the impending disaster he had stayed away; and now, in response to the sarcastic cries of "author! author!" he was led on stage by the vengeful Alexander. What happened next can best be described in James's own words:

> There followed an abominable quarter of an hour during which all the forces of civilisation in the house waged a battle of the most gallant, prolonged and sustained applause with the hoots and jeers and catcalls of the roughs whose *roars* (like those of caged beasts at some infernal "zoo") were only exacerbated (as it were) by the conflict. It was a cheering scene, as you may imagine, for a nervous, sensitive, exhausted author to face—and you must spare my going over again that horrid hour, or those of disappointment and depression that have followed it . . .

The experience—how could it be otherwise?—was nothing less than traumatic. His novels had failed but his plays were a catastrophe. It was the period of lowest ebb in his far from dazzling career.

James sat down at his desk and took stock of his situation. His self-confidence, though shaken, was by no means shattered; he resolved to return to writing fiction. In January, 1895, soon after the debacle of *Guy Domville*, he recorded in his notebooks:

> I take up my *own* old pen again—the pen of all my old unforgettable efforts and sacred struggles. To myself—today—I need say no more. Large and full and high the future still opens. It is now indeed that I may do the work of my life. And I will.

He attempted thoroughly to reappraise his narrative approach, and concluded that the major flaw in his earlier work was his fatal tendency to expansion, dilation and length. Towards the end of January he wrote to Howells: "I shall never again write a *long* novel, but I hope to write six immortal short ones—and some tales of the same quality." During the next few weeks, while he was settling down to work on these shorter projects, it gradually dawned on him that what he had learned as a playwright might be relevant to his work as a novelist. James's mounting excitement, as he realised the stylistic potentials involved, is both moving and infectious:

> *Voyons, voyons:* may I not instantly sit down to a little, close, clear full scenario of it? As I ask myself the question, *with* the very asking of it, and the utterance of that word so charged with memories and pains, something seems to open out before me, and at the same time to press upon me with an extraordinary tenderness of embrace. Compensations and solutions seem to stand there with open arms for me—and something of the "meaning" to come to me of past bitterness, of recent bitterness that otherwise has seemed a mere sickening, unflavoured draught. Has *part* of all this wasted passion and squandered time (of the last 5 years) been simply the precious lesson, taught me in that roundabout and devious way, *of the singular value for a narrative plan too* of the (I don't know what adequately to call it) divine principle of the Scenario? If that *has* been one side of the moral of the whole unspeakable, the whole tragic experience, I almost bless the pangs and pains and the miseries of it. IF there has lurked in the central core of it this

exquisite truth—I almost hold my breath with suspense as I try to formulate it; so much, so *much* hangs radiantly there as depending on it—this exquisite truth that what I call the divine principle in question is a key that, working in the same general way, fits the complicated chambers of both the dramatic and narrative lock: IF, I say, I have crept round through long apparent barrenness, through suffering and sadness intolerable, to that rare perception—why my infinite little loss is converted into an almost infinite little gain.

We should be clear as to the nature of James's discovery in this passage. He has not stumbled, after twenty years as a novelist, on the necessity to plan his stories in advance. What he conceives instead is the possibility of the novel as play; of a narrative action built in scenic blocks. The divine principle of the scenario is the divine principle of scenic design: fiction conceived and executed in single-scene capsules and rendered, so far as possible, according to a dramatic analogy with all the objectivity, economy and visibility of the theatre at maximum narrative stretch. Thus James hoped to give his work the brevity, intensity and impact which would guarantee its immortality; and achieve all this without having to sacrifice any of his earlier narrative goals.

The transition from the novelist as painter to the novelist as dramatist was not, however, quite as abrupt as my account has suggested. The scissile possibilities of dramatic method and theatrical actuality had been hovering on the fringes of James's mind for some time; certainly for more than a year before his discovery of the scenario principle he was capable of separating the notion of the drama from the idea of the theatre. Towards the end of 1894, for example, he remarked in a letter, "I may have been meant for the Drama—God knows!—but I certainly wasn't meant for the Theatre." Even more revealingly, he wrote to William in 1893:

> The whole odiousness of the thing lies in the connection between the drama and the theatre. The one is admirable in its interest and difficulty, the other loathsome in its conditions. If the drama could only be theoretically or hypothetically acted, the fascination resident in its all but unconquerable (*circumspice!*) form would be unimpaired and one would be able to have the exquisite exercise without the horrid sacrifice.

When, on St Valentine's Day, 1895, he hit upon the obvious solution to the problem, he found that he was able to put it into practice almost immediately. His grasp of the technicalities of play construction, unquestionably, was more than adequate. Twelve days before, on February 2, he had written to William defending his grasp of dramatic method; quite naturally, in the face of the disaster which had overtaken *Guy Domville*, William had questioned his competence as dramatic technician. Henry's reply, however, was an interesting one: that he had failed in the theatre not through too little concern for technique but through too much. His mastery of the form, he said, had led to a fatal neglect of what he called "the question of subject." The implication of this is clear. James, returning to the narrative form in this frame of mind, was resolved to exploit his grasp of dramatic technique together with a fresh emphasis on subject.

Eighteen ninety-five, then, is the pivotal year in James's artistic evolution. His commitment to what he later called "intense illusion"—his sense that the object of literature was the communication through artistic legerdemain of an impression of life's infinite complexities—resolved itself ultimately into the conviction that dramatic representation was the technical solution for which he sought. He was drawn to the theatre, and later to experimentation in his novels with dramatic method, because the theatrical form appeared to synthesise his aesthetic aspirations. It provided at the same time a coherent technical procedure which he was able to reconcile with his earlier aesthetic goals—the portrait, the accurately observed contemporary fact, the effacement of the omniscient narrator and so on. During the next phase of his career—his most fecund period—the dramatic simile proved to be a fertile technical resource for further additions to his aesthetic. In novels such as *The Awkward Age* and *What Maisie Knew*, for instance, the emphases on dialogue, compact, tightly-structured action, and temporal foreshortening, bear an obvious relationship to the new analogy; while elsewhere his experimentation with the central reflecting consciousness, in *The Sacred Fount*, for instance, or *The Ambassadors*, evolved from his earlier interest in the role of the audience.

But here we come to a central difficulty. It is of course true that, for all the reasons we have already outlined, James was pro-

26

foundly attracted to the theatre and dramatic form; but it is
equally true—and here the difficulty arises—that when he first
began to compose dramas for the London stage, he cherished a
supreme contempt for the sort of thing he was going to have to
write. In 1889 the renaissance of the British theatre was barely
under way; the example of Sardoodledum, of the Scribean *pièce
bien faite*, still reigned supreme. Within the framework of its
trivial formulae, as James well understood, genuine innovation and
real dramatic art were not possible. Its conventions were designed
to permit a high degree of humorous predictability and agreeable
falsity to enter the action; in its characteristic form (the French
bedroom comedy) the well-made play deployed witty prose dialogue, a stolidly upper-bourgeois setting, adultery invariably as a
topic, disguise, mistaken identity and, above all, as a method for
sustaining action and suspense, the adventures of incriminating but
perpetually mislaid letters. (A. B. Walkley once wickedly remarked
that Sardou's penchant for this device was indeed his only claim
to being a man of letters.) Serious characterisation was seldom
attempted; the conventions of the genre demanded that only
stereotypes be employed—the Cuckold Husband, the Saucy Maid,
the Knowing Butler. And the whole dish was served up, as James
himself contemptuously observed, "with the time-honoured bread-
sauce of the happy ending."

In other words, the *pièce bien faite* was a vehicle for the after-
dinner amusement of the affluent middle classes. Its modest goal
was frivolous entertainment; its essence was froth and its claims
consciously ephemeral. Sardou and Scribe, the two supreme prac-
titioners of the form, produced between themselves nearly one
thousand of these airy, post-prandial amusettes; and in not one
of them is there a serious thought. Quite consciously so too; for
as Scribe explained in a speech to the French Academy in 1836,
it was falsity alone which amused his audience; the truth merely
depressed them.

From what we have already noted about James's Realist ambitions, the extraordinary violence he was doing to himself by elect-
ing, at least in the first instance, to work within this sterile
tradition, should be obvious. Furthermore he was fully aware of
the artistic wilderness to which he was condemning himself. When
he set out to dramatise *The American* in 1889 he invoked scorn-

fully the great names of contemporary French drama: "Oh, how it must not be too good and how very bad it must be! *A moi*, Scribe; *à moi*, Sardou; *à moi*, Dennery!" He was setting out, quite deliberately, as he later observed, to make a sow's ear out of a silk purse; and this of course is one of the reasons for the failure of his dramas.

But if all this is true; if, that is to say, the drama specifically controverted his most profoundly cherished artistic goals, how and why did James come to surrender his portrait metaphor in exchange for one drawn from the drama when he returned to the 'other ink' of narrative prose in the winter of 1895?

The answer lies largely in his encounter with the work of Henrik Ibsen, the great Norwegian playwright whose bitter prose tragedies were revolutionising the British theatre precisely during the period of James's most energetic bid for dramatic success. In 1889, the year James committed himself fully to writing for the stage, an extraordinary literary storm, unique in its intensity, virulence and brevity, broke about the heads of Ibsen and his supporters in England.[1] His plays were denounced as disgusting, obscene and immoral; the man himself was a corruptor of innocents and virgins, a purveyor of sex, socialism and feminine emancipation. The screams of rage and the demands for censorship increased in proportion as Ibsen's real greatness became apparent; and ceased just as abruptly when his genius was established beyond dispute. Within four years the force of Ibsen's consistent brilliance—and the eloquence of his supporters, of whom James was one—completely transformed the London stage. By June, 1893, when Beerbohm Tree triumphed with his production of *An Enemy of the People*, the sterile hold which the Scribean form had exercised for so long was broken.

James's conversion to Ibsen, as we shall see in the course of this book, was by no means immediate. He was, as we all are, the product of his age; and though he scorned the Scribean genre his assumptions about what a dramatist could and should attempt were shaped by his experience of the Paris stage. His early attitude to Ibsen was thus remorselessly hostile. As he grew acquainted

[1] I have discussed this period in greater detail in my introduction to *Henrik Ibsen: The Critical Heritage* (Routledge & Kegan Paul, 1972). Apart from other documents relevant to Ibsen's reception, the book includes some previously unpublished letters by James to Gosse about Ibsen, as well as all of James's commentaries.

with the plays, however, and particularly after he saw them in production, he became increasingly enthusiastic. By 1891, following the première of *Hedda Gabler*, he had become one of Ibsen's most prestigious supporters.

What James learned finally and particularly to admire in Ibsen was his ability to achieve in the drama precisely what the well-made play refused to do. We have noted that the French constructionists specifically turned their faces from contemporary social fact, arguing that, so far as they and their audiences were concerned, falsity alone was amusing. But Ibsen switched the thing about, writing plays which, in their dogged insistence on the actualities of nineteenth-century Europe, were the polar opposite of ephemeral drawing-room comedies. They were in fact drawing-room tragedies. Ibsen showed James not only that the theatre *should* be used as a vehicle for serious social comment, like the novel, but that modern drama *could* sustain intense investigations of character and situation, of states of mind and soul. James discovered through Ibsen that Realism, to which he was of course committed as a novelist, was not antipathetic to the drama, as he had originally believed. Later, after he had acknowledged, at least to himself, his failure as a dramatist, he began to bring into his narrative work many of the aesthetic and technical assumptions he had found in Ibsen's drama. The most far-reaching consequence of this importation was his gradual assimilation of Ibsen's symbolic manner: the golden bowl was struck in Norway. At the core of my study is the argument that it was Ibsen who showed James how to use Hawthorne.

If one compares James's late critique of Flaubert with his attitude to Ibsen at approximately the same period, many of these points emerge forcefully. Flaubert was, James came to feel—and the shift in emphasis is of course significant—essentially a novelist of externalities. He begins "on the outside"—and there he sticks. He notes the surface actualities of life effectively enough, but fails to penetrate to its essence. For the younger James the Flaubertian manner represented the apex of the novelist's art: *Madame Bovary* is the ideal early James fiction and Flaubert the supreme portraitist. But for the later James, the James of the post-theatre period, Flaubert's realism, although a considerable achievement, was simply superficial. It presented life as "before all things a spectacle, an occupation and entertainment for the eyes." Now Ibsen's power, on the other hand, lay precisely in his capacity to penetrate that outer surface, to pierce spectacle and communicate triumphantly his sense of what James called, in a review of *Hedda Gabler*, "the passions, the idiosyncrasies, the cupidities and jealousies, the strivings and struggles, the joys and sufferings of men. The spectator's situation is different enough when what is given him is the mere dead rattle of the surface of life into which *he* has to inject the element of thought, the 'human interest'. Ibsen kneads the soul of man like a paste . . ." He succeeded in conveying the pure and intense sense of "felt life", and achieved it all within a triumphant mastery of dramatic technique. Ibsen possessed "a real method" and had "mastered an exceedingly difficult form." All these factors working together meant that he was able to effect "the ticklish transfusion of life" into his art—life as it was experienced by real people in a real nineteenth-century world.

Throughout the rest of his career, then, as this study will seek to show, James experimented continuously in his novels and tales with dramatic method and ideas and techniques drawn either directly from Ibsen's plays or from the ethos of the style of theatre he created. In *The Spoils of Poynton* and *The Other House*, for instance, both of which date from the immediate post-theatre period of 1895–6, Ibsen's shaping presence is particularly noticeable. *The Other House*, as Pelham Edgar remarked nearly forty years ago, reads like an Ibsen play "with Jamesian amplifications"; and many critics since have traced its strong dependence on *Hedda Gabler* and *Rosmersholm*. *The Spoils of Poynton*, modelled quite explicitly on a dramatic analogy, according to James himself, was also profoundly affected by *Rosmersholm*. In addition *The Master Builder* appears to have exerted some sort of pressure on James's conception of the central figures and the predicaments they face.

During the next few years Ibsen's drama continued to make itself crucially felt in James's work. The high points of its influence are to be found particularly among the nouvelles, and especially in such works as *Covering End* and *The Turn of the Screw* (which seems to me to be deeply indebted to *Ghosts*). These peaks, however, of course suggest valleys, usually discoverable among the short stories; nevertheless throughout this period—that is, up to about 1900—there is a certain unity of thematic concern, apart

30

from the continual experimentation with dramatic method, which relates it directly to Ibsen. To put it another way, James's encounter with Ibsen made novels like *What Maisie Knew* (1897) and *The Awkward Age* (1899) possible. The theme of corrupt innocence, the main idea underpinning these works, was not of course a new one for James; yet we are I think right to follow Edmund Wilson at this point and distinguish *The American* or *The Portrait of a Lady* from the novels of absolute evil and sexual corruption which characterise the later period. The violation of childish innocence in a depraved environment where the conditions of family life are sordid in the extreme—this theme, which we encounter again and again in James's later work, clearly owes at least something to the general exemplative pressure created by (say) *Little Eyolf*, *Ghosts*, and *The Wild Duck*.

During this period in James's career, therefore, the change in aesthetic metaphor from the portrait to the drama was completed and confirmed. But James did not stop there. Again, one of the reasons for the failure of his plays was that, ultimately, he was interested in what was happening in the drama *below* the surface, that is, in what was going on in the minds of his protagonists, rather than in the superficialities of plot and action. Thus gradually as he extended the metaphor of the theatre in his later work his emphasis began to fall increasingly on what was happening within rather than without; that is to say, he began to dramatise consciousness. This passage from his notebook preparations for *The Spoils of Poynton* illustrates the point vividly:

. . . I mustn't interrupt it too much with elucidations or it will be interminable. IT MUST BE AS STRAIGHT AS A PLAY—that is the only way to do. Ah, *mon bon*, make *this*, *here*, justify, crown, in its little degree, the long years and pains, the acquired mastery of scenic presentation. What I am looking for is my joint, my hinge, for making the scene between them pass, at a given point, into passion, into pain, into their facing together the truth. Some point that it logically reaches must DETERMINE the passage. I want to give Fleda her little hour. She can only *get* it if Owen fully comes out. Owen can only fully come out if he sees what is really in her. He must offer to give up Mona for her—and she must utterly refuse that. What her response IS is that she will take him if Mona really breaks. Yes, here I get my evolution don't I?—an understanding between them dependent on the things not coming . . .

What is happening here is that James is passing over from the dramatisation of events to the dramatisation of states of mind and soul, the conditions of what is happening below the surface of the dialogue and the action. His continued evolution in this direction resulted finally in the complex evocations of consciousness so characteristic of the novels of the major phase.

There is one last important point to bear in mind. As a young man—and his early study of Hawthorne substantiates this—he had deeply mistrusted symbolism and allegory. He believed that they subverted the accurate portrayal of contemporary reality; that their premises, precisely, distanced both author and reader from the actual. But Ibsen showed James, contrary to his original assumptions, that symbolism and realism were not necessarily in conflict, that the former could be employed to heighten the latter. Ibsen's technique was to create a fabric of closely interwoven images which were allowed to interact, at key moments, with the physical worlds in which his protagonists lived and died. In *Rosmersholm*, for example, a vivid sequence of water imagery unites with the action at a critical juncture when Rosmer and Rebecca go to their deaths in the mill-race. Or, to take another instance, in *Hedda Gabler* images of fire and burning located in the early scenes leap into life at the central moment when Hedda burns Eilert Lövborg's manuscript, infusing the action with an intensity of horror, a kind of hyper-reality.

It was this technique, perhaps above all others, which James began to borrow from Ibsen during the post-theatre phase. As his later manner developed it became increasingly important in his work so that, in the novels and stories of the final years, we may say that it is the major vehicle of the action. In a novel like *The Ambassadors*, for instance, the chief impact lies simply in the interaction of, again, persistent water imagery and crucial active moments. Both working in conjunction serve to invest the whole novel with a sense of vast, almost mythic pressures locked in elephantine combat.

And so we come round again to the problem of James's later manner as posed in the passage from *The Golden Bowl* which I quoted earlier. James's movement, as I have argued, is reflected in his evolving aesthetic metaphor, a progress from the spectator "out there", objectively viewing the Renaissance portrait—a two-dimensional approach—to the spectator (that is, the reader) within the portrait itself, looking back as it were on his own world through the portrait's eyes. But the analogy is of course that of the drama, the drama of consciousness, enveloped in highly intense symbolic parameters derived, in the first instance, from Ibsen. James achieved this movement, from "out there" to "in here", without feeling for a moment that he had ever sacrificed his fundamental commitment to Realism, the accurate presentation of life as he saw it to be.

PART ONE

Henry James and Ibsen

1

The Initial Impact

From first to last James's reactions to Ibsen were marked by a strange irresolution, an attitude of halting deference which swung between masochistic submission and violent hostility. Even his earliest comments, written before he had read so much as a line of the Norwegian's work, are touched with ambiguity and a kind of shy hope. He first heard of Ibsen early in 1889, soon after completing *The Tragic Muse* and, as it were, in the very act of putting pen to paper to write his first mature play. Towards the end of January that year his friend Edmund Gosse, for nearly twenty years Ibsen's most vocal advocate in England, published one of his militantly campaigning pieces in *The Fortnightly Review*.[1] A few days later James wrote to him: "I have perused your very interesting account of Ibsen, as I always peruse you when I find you. You must tell me more about I. That is not in this case female-American for *me*." The curious, and yet clearly not wholly unconscious, linguistic identification with Ibsen which James permits himself in this odd passage, was one which he was subsequently to repeat. In December, 1896, for example, many years after he had surrendered to what he called the "hard compulsion" of Ibsen's "strangely inscrutable art", he wrote to the actress Elizabeth Robins: "What an old boy is our Northern Henry!—he is too delightful—an old darling!" Yet the lyricism of this last and by no means untypical passage was not to endure into the Prefaces, when he allowed himself some strange and oddly ambiguous comments in the Introduction to *The Awkward Age*. And again, one wonders—in this instance as in so many

[1] Gosse's article is reprinted in *Henrik Ibsen: The Critical Heritage*.

others—for whose eyes precisely this exuberant passage from the notebooks was intended:

> I realise—none too soon—that the *scenic* method is my absolute, my imperative, my *only* salvation. The *march of an action* is the thing for me to, more and more, *attach* myself to: it is the only thing that really, for *me*, at least, will *produire* L'OEUVRE, and L'OEUVRE is, before God, what I'm going in for. Well, the scenic scheme is the only one that *I* can trust, with my tendencies to stick to the march of an action. How reading Ibsen's splendid *John Gabriel* a day or two ago (in proof) brought that FINALLY AND FOREVER, home to me!

There seems little doubt, however, despite repeated passages like these in his letters and elsewhere, that James's conversion to Ibsenism, at least in the Shavian sense, was never permanent. Ibsen—his own, very personal view of Ibsen—came upon him in successive waves, touching now this work, now that, leaving others relatively unmarked. At other times, especially in the early years of his encounter with the Ibsen theatre, he was capable of imitation for the most commercial of reasons. We may take those muffled echoes of Ibsen to be found in the dramatised version of *The American* for instance (a contemporary reviewer said that Elizabeth Robins, playing Madame de Cintre, imported to the play "the hysterical manners of Ibsen's morbid heroines") as constituting the shallowest form of gesture to theatre fashion.

Henry James, we have already noted, first became interested in Ibsen in January, 1889. We can infer from his letters, furthermore, that Gosse replied to his request for additional information with a flood of books, translations and articles—the first of a sustained and ultimately successful effort to win James's public support for Ibsen. Initially, however, he failed and, as Elizabeth Robins testifies in *Theatre and Friendship*, her fascinating and invaluable memoir of James's involvement in the Ibsen movement, James made at this point no effort to acquaint himself further with Ibsen's work. No more requests for books followed and James, perhaps feeling that Ibsen was too far outside the mainstream of European drama to be of use to him, stolidly ignored both the productions of Ibsen dramas which were taking place in London (Janet Achurch's historic *A Doll's House* in June, 1889, and *The Pillars of Society* in July) and the astonishing furore in

the press which they provoked. The earliest record we thus have
of his attending a production occurs in 1891, when he asked Mrs
Genevieve Ward to take him to the revival of *A Doll's House* at
Terry's Theatre on January 27. It is likely, however, that even at
this juncture his interest was less in Ibsen than in the players—
Elizabeth Robins, whom he had met a few days earlier during
rehearsal, was playing Mrs Linde and James had her in mind for
the female lead in *The American*. She notes that he had read at
least *Hedda Gabler* by this time, quoting a letter which he wrote
to Mrs Hugh Bell in which he urged her to read the play "for its
strange mixture of pointless flatness and convincing *life*. Also of
desolate untheatricality and dramatic ingenuity." Again that
characteristically ambivalent, almost contradictory, response: initially, James was completely bewildered by Ibsen.

The late winter and spring of 1891 saw the height of the Ibsen
controversy in England. Between February and May, a matter of
ten weeks, *Rosmersholm, Ghosts, Hedda Gabler* and *The Lady
from the Sea* were all premièred. The bitterness and hostility, and
the verbal hysteria ("muck-ferreting dogs . . . a dirty act done
publicly", etc.) are now matters of literary history. By the time *The
Lady from the Sea* was produced in May London was glutted with
Ibsen and the arguments over his immorality or greatness. On the
other hand, and this was obviously more important, it was also
clear to all but his most vociferous opponents, such as the
waspish Clement Scott, theatre critic for the nation's largest-
circulation newspaper, *The Daily Telegraph*, that he was a major
talent and no passing fashion. The spring of 1891, as I have argued
elsewhere, was perhaps the most momentous period in the history
of the modern British theatre. It is a comment on James of the
most extraordinary kind, as his letters to Gosse bear out, that,
except in one instance, he made no effort to attend any of these
remarkable performances.

On the other hand the one that he did go to, the première of
Hedda Gabler on April 20, ultimately wrought a revolution in his
attitude towards Ibsen. It is ironic that he probably attended it
more in a spirit of friendly loyalty to Elizabeth Robins, who
had co-produced it with Marion Lea and was starring in it, than
out of professional curiosity. Six weeks later, however, when he
published his long defence of the play in the *New Review*—and

Hedda Gabler needed defending: it had been sharply attacked—
he emerged finally as one of Ibsen's most influential and articu-
late supporters in England. He was declaring publicly, at the very
height of the debate, his intention of making common cause on
Ibsen's behalf with Gosse, Symons, Archer, George Moore, Have-
lock Ellis, Bernard Shaw and almost every other literary figure of
note at the time. Thus, although James was never to play a leading
or even decisive role in the struggle for Ibsen in England, his
declaration of allegiance at this juncture—and of course the force
of his critical intelligence—effectively silenced all opposition to
Hedda Gabler itself. His coolly considered analysis, judiciously
evaluating Ibsen's remarkable gifts and occasional deficiencies,
was unanswerable.

It should not however be thought that as James sat in the stalls
watching *Hedda Gabler* he experienced some kind of Damascan
illumination in which he suddenly perceived the error of his former
ways. What struck him most forcefully at first was that he had
perhaps been premature in his rejection of Ibsen; that there was
a serious and significant disparity between his experience as
reader and his response as viewer. This was one of the first points
he made in his review of the play:

> We have studied our author, it must be admitted, under diffi-
> culties, for it is impossible not to read him without perceiving that
> merely book in hand we but half know him—he addresses himself
> so substantially to representation . . . The stage is to the prose
> drama (and Ibsen's later manner is the very prose of prose) what
> the tune is to the song or the concrete case to the general law. It
> immediately becomes apparent that he needs the test to show
> his strength and the frame to show his picture. An extraordinary
> vivification takes place; the conditions seem essentially enlarged . . .
> [*Hedda Gabler*], on perusal, left one completely muddled and mysti-
> fied, fascinated but—in one's intellectual sympathy—snubbed.
> Acted, it leads that sympathy over the straightest of roads with all
> the exhilaration of a superior pace.

Yet even this experience was not immediately decisive. He had
been re-reading Ibsen, by way of preparation for the general sur-
vey which he included in his account of *Hedda Gabler* in June,
and had found himself remorselessly and embarrassingly driven
back to his original conclusion: Ibsen was profoundly mediocre.

More than a week after seeing *Hedda Gabler*, on April 28, he wrote
to Edmund Gosse admitting as much. Gosse had sent him a fresh
volume of translations, prepared for an American audience,[1]
which included a lengthy preface by himself based on the *Fortnightly Review* article which had first caught James's attention.
James returned "the Ibsenite volume" with thanks and then went
on to confess that try as he might he was unable to see any merit
in Ibsen at all. *Ghosts* and *Rosmersholm*, in particular, struck him
as being of a "grey mediocrity—in the case of *Rosmersholm
jusqu'a en être bête*." His major objection at this stage was not
that Ibsen's plays were immoral, the usual philistine objection,
but that on the contrary they were only too tediously moralising
and that, in consequence, they failed as dramas. He went on:

> They don't seem to me dramatic or dramas at all—but (I am
> speaking of these two particularly) moral tales in dialogue without
> the objectivity, the visibility of the drama. They suggest curious
> reflections as to the Scandinavian stage and audience. Of course
> they have a serious—a terribly serious "feeling for life" and always
> an idea—but they come off so little, in general as plays; and I can't
> think that a man who is at odds with his form is ever a first rate
> man. But I may be grossly blind; and at any rate don't tell it of yours
> tremulously, Henry James.

The terms of James's early hostility are valid enough, so long
as one grants the Scribean premises on which they are based.
Indeed, in an oblique way, they reflect a continuing problem in
Ibsen criticism. And yet at the same time they point the way to
his eventual acceptance of Ibsen as a major dramatic talent, since
it is clear that even at this stage he had grasped something of
Ibsen's deep ethical preoccupations and concern with dramatic
realism. During the next four or five weeks he undertook a complete reappraisal of Ibsen and his contribution to dramatic form;
and at the end of this period he was prepared to announce himself
publicly an Ibsenist. That his praise was not unqualified is com-
prehensible in view of what we know of his early bafflement;
nevertheless the fact that he eventually came down quite firmly
on Ibsen's side is a remarkable tribute to his own intellectual in-

---

[1] *Lovell's Series of Foreign Literature: The Prose Dramas of Henrik Ibsen.*
Vol. 1: *A Doll's House, The Pillars of Society, Ghosts, Rosmersholm.*
With an Introduction by Edmund Gosse (New York and Boston, 1890).

tegrity. "On the Occasion of *Hedda Gabler*" is a piece which bears all the marks of hard work, hard reading and the most rigorous thought. *The Reprobate*, the play on which he was working at this time, and on which he continued to work throughout the summer and early autumn of 1891, was, as a result and as we shall see, the first of his creative writings to bear significant traces of Ibsen's exemplative imprint.

James's review of *Hedda Gabler* (in point of fact the first part of a long study of Ibsen which he was to complete in 1893 and publish as a whole in his *Essays in London and Elsewhere*) is symmetrically arranged in balancing and contrasting sections. On the one hand we have James, speaking in his guise as the English Sardou, ticking off Ibsen's personal and dramatic deficiencies: his want of humour, of playfulness, of free imagination. In addition, says James, Ibsen is inclined to exaggerate somewhat—"he makes his heredity too short and the consequences too long"—and is occasionally tempted, as in *The Lady from the Sea*, to deal with pettiness of motive. Finally, he rather gratuitously indulges in outraging Victorian social convention: "he actually talks of stockings and legs, in addition to other improprieties." James does not, however, take Ibsen to task for this; on the contrary, his mocking tone is aimed directly at English prurience. But—and commercial considerations were important to James at this time—he felt quite genuinely that it was this sort of unnecessary challenge which would ensure Ibsen's continuing unpopularity with the London *bildungspöbel* and condemn him to perpetual box-office failure.

On the other hand, however, there was Ibsen's unique achievement in having discovered a dramatic method whereby the illusion of life, the ambiguity and complexity of human personality, might be portrayed on stage. Ibsen had created a style of drama which could substitute character, intension, states of soul, for frothy action and the glittering surfaces of plot. Paradoxically, or so it seemed to James, this supreme accomplishment emerged, precisely, from Ibsen's deficiencies. His "infinitely noted . . . recurrent ugliness of surface" and relentless concentration on the charmless details of bourgeois provinciality, permitted him an intensity and power which, though a little clumsy in action, more than compensated for the loss of fantasy and idealisation. Ibsen—

this is the perception, I think, towards which James was moving—
had brought the aesthetics of Realism into the theatre. He had
created the middle-class drawing-room tragedy. By his unswerving
"fidelity to the real" he had discovered an effective substitute for
the charm of the Scribean genre.

> This it is that brings us back to the author's great quality, the
> quality that makes him so interesting in spite of his limitations, so
> rich in spite of his lapses—his habit of dealing essentially with the
> individual caught in the fact.

When he turned to consider *Hedda Gabler* itself James found it
a superb example of Ibsen's realist art. It was the product of a
mind "saturated, above all, with a sense of the infinitude, for all
its mortal savour, of *character*." Ibsen's unique ability lay in his
power to create not the mimesis of a praxis but "that supposedly
undramatic thing, the picture not of an action but of a condition." *Hedda Gabler* was

> the portrait of a nature, the story of what Paul Bourget would call
> an *état d'âme*, and of a state of nerves as well as of soul, a state of
> temper, of health, of chagrin, of despair.

He was struck by Ibsen's capacity to attempt so theatrically un-
promising a thing and still succeed in making it live "with the
intensity of life." This was the highest praise James could bestow.
The power to create a sense of life's limitless complexities was a
"grace", as he later expressed it in his Preface to *The Ambassadors*,
to which the intelligent writer will, "at any time, for his interest,
sacrifice if need be all other graces whatever." Thus Ibsen became
for him the supreme artistic creator. He "kneads the soul of man
like a paste", charging his dramatic canvas with moral colour and
firmly-lined characterisation. The "shapely" *Pillars of Society*, for
instance, "with its large, dense complexity of moral cross-refer-
ences and its admirable definiteness as a picture of motive and
temperament . . . asks the average moral man to see many things
at once."

This was not a style of drama to which James, as yet, felt inclined to commit himself personally. He believed, with justification, that it was after all the average moral man who sat in most
of the theatre stalls, and that, further, it was precisely Ibsen's dour
refusal to court such an individual with humour and light-hearted

irrelevancies which was one explanation for the negative spirit in which his productions to date had been received. This was why he continued to think it necessary at this time to flatter the sensibilities of his own (putative) audiences with frivolous and improbable fantasies in the manner of Sardou; and why, too, he felt with some misgivings that Ibsen's intellectual demands, although clearly a source of artistic strength, were too great. Average moral men resist complexities.

At the same time, however, we can, by employing a degree of hindsight, detect James in this review plotting for himself his future theatre strategy. What he sees to be of use in Ibsen—the delineation of character, for example—he immediately subsumes; where he feels a necessary quality to be lacking—the absence of humour, for instance—he resolves to supply it; that which cannot be exploited—Ibsen's moral turgidity—he immediately rejects. It was the beginning of a long process of assimilation which ultimately transformed James's entire vision of the dramatist's art.

James understood perfectly well that it was not Ibsen who was at fault but his public. "If we possessed the unattainable," he concluded, "an electic, artistic, disinterested theatre to which we might look for alteration and variety, it would simply be a point of honour in such a temple to sacrifice sometimes to Henrik Ibsen." And it was in this cynical frame of mind that he continued to work on *The Reprobate*. From his remarks it should be clear what he was about to attempt: the portrait of a nature, of a condition, but sugared with a liberal dose of humour and free imagination. He was about to undertake his first sacrifice to the Ibsen idol. His offerings, initially, were timid and severely limited; he did not wish to court Ibsen's unpopularity, only his success. Later, when Ibsen had become more respectable, and James had come to understand with greater clarity the magnitude of his achievement, there followed plays—for example, *The Other House*—which sought to emulate him in all particulars. In *The Reprobate*, however, he was still inhibited and afraid, still the apprentice playwright, and so contented himself with smaller gestures.

Small gestures, perhaps, but significant nevertheless. *The Reprobate* is a study of an individual "caught in the fact"; it is the "portrait of a nature, the story of what Paul Bourget would call an *état d'âme*." In no sense whatever could any of James's earlier dramas be described in these terms. *The Album*, for instance, the play which preceded *The Reprobate* by a few months—but written before James undertook his reappraisal of Ibsen—bears this out to the full. It is a typically Scribean comedy. Action and plot are coterminous, character is subordinate to the exigencies of the tale, incident and coincidence are supreme. Interest focuses on the event and dramatic suspense, such as it is, derives from the caprices of chance or character or the manipulated adventures (like Sardou's letters) of the eponymous album. But in *The Reprobate* the dramatic structure is no longer that of the French clock-work comedy. The story deals with a crisis in the life of an individual caught up in an ironic and (relatively) powerful situation rendered complex by serious moral undertones. While there is plot, that is to say, there is very little action: characteristically Ibsen.

Paul Doubleday is the hero of *The Reprobate*. Though thirty years old and intelligent, he is treated by his immediate family as though he were a deficient child. His liberty is curtailed in all things. His keepers, for they are no less, are his stepmother and his dead father's close friend, Mr Bonsor. This tyranny over Paul's individuality is exercised in the name of his moral welfare.

Into this situation James introduces two women, Blanche Amber and Nina Freshville, who together achieve Paul's personal salvation by encouraging him to defy his family. Through his liberation they bring about the redemption of the claustrophobic community which represses him, for Paul liberated, like Paul enchained, is a symbol of the passions. What happens in the play is largely what happens in the psyche of the hero. As we have noted, it is effectively the portrait and analysis of a condition, the study of a state of soul and of a personality in crisis. Paul Doubleday *is* the play. Act I describes the conditions of his moral and physical confinement; Act II his growing sense of injustice, his realisation that he is not the slave of reprehensible passions and that, therefore, he need acquiesce no longer in his situation; Act III the smashing of the bonds, Prometheus unbound. This image is not gratuitous. Blanche makes the reference when she says to Paul: "I want you living; I want you fluttering; I want you perched on your rock, at least, if you must be tied to it . . . I'll stay as long as you hold out."

As this speech indicates, James was by no means unaware of the tragic implications of his play: Paul is the victim of a monstrous egotism. But, bearing in mind his critique of Ibsen's moral ponderousness, and remembering the average moral men sitting in the stalls, he sheered away from too profound a probing of the issues raised. *The Reprobate* remains a comedy. From time to time, however, James permitted exchanges such as this to take place:

> Blanche: [impressed, taking it very seriously] You live, then, in such terror?
>
> Paul: Not quite in terror, perhaps, but in very great anxiety. I never know what I may do next.
>
> Blanche: [smiling] You frighten *me* a little!
>
> Paul: Oh, now that I've explained, I shall again put on the mask.
>
> Blanche: [sighing] The tragic mask!
>
> Paul: Not even that: the expressionless.

In the figure of Paul Doubleday James created for the first time in a drama a hero who existed in depth and in a situation of moral complexity. Paul is a protagonist involved in a serious and, with a a slight change in emphasis, very nearly tragic fact. He is about to be plunged into the crisis of his life, and he responds to it in a manner reminiscent of Ibsen's early heroines. In particular terms—it is clear even from the brief description of his situation which I have just offered—his plight approximates too closely for coincidence to the predicaments confronting both Nora Helmer in *A Doll's House* and Dina Dorf in *The Pillars of Society*. I shall of course be coming back to this point presently.

The Reprobate, then, deals with the titanic and inexorable pressures which a decadent but powerful community can exert upon the individual. James's oblique point is that if a man remains true to himself, expresses his innermost nature, he will be able to resist them and break their power. In order to defeat and expose their hollowness, however, he must persist in his fidelity to his real self. This notion alone relates the play powerfully to Ibsen. But corollary to this theme and underpinning it—and the note James sounds at this point should alert us immediately to the possibility of a borrowing from Ibsen—is the idea that an individual's moral worth and strength are determined by genetic inheritance and the ethos of early childhood. It is an assumption that clearly derives from

Ibsen. Not only does it permeate his prose dramas; and not only was it the aspect of his work which most upset many of his critics; but—and this is crucial—it has no precedence in any of James's earlier work. Ibsen's positivist theories about inheritance, heredity and moral debt, placed at the very centre of a Henry James play, are important trace elements indicating the presence of a new orientation.

In *The Reprobate*, and James makes the point repeatedly, it is heredity which determines ultimately one's moral condition: whether one is natural, spontaneous, committed to life and honest passion, like Paul, or whether, like Mrs Doubleday and Mr Bonsor, one is dulled and choked, a hypocritical hater of youthful *joie de vivre*. Early in the play, for example, Paul is discussed in geneological terms clearly deriving from Ibsen's widely-debated notion of moral inheritance. Mrs Doubleday, Paul's stepmother, (the point is made several times) explains to the prurient Captain Chanter that Paul's dissolute nature is a trait inherited directly from his mother, an "indelicate" woman. The Captain replies that he can judge well enough "of the blood that flows in Paul's veins." The exchange continues:

> Mrs Doubleday: Heredity, heredity! My husband's favourite expression. He saw it bear dreadful fruit.
> Chanter: From the child's earliest years?
> Mrs Doubleday: Almost from the cradle.

James's intention, of course, is to suggest a meaning opposite to Mrs Doubleday's: Paul is full of life and joy. Nevertheless he stands by the genetic mechanism. Later he returns to it and develops it in a subsequent exchange. Here Mrs Doubleday is explaining to Chanter that she has no living children of her own:

> Mrs Doubleday: . . . I presented [the late Mr Doubleday] with a second son who, alas, didn't live.
> Chanter: If he had, he too would have been faultless.
> Mrs Doubleday: Heredity again!

James had fully grasped Ibsen's idea. The notion of genetic inheritance is a real force in the play and not simply a verbal decoration or gesture towards theatrical fashion. Moral conditions are indeed inherited; and the ugly, tyrannical Mrs Doubleday can give life to nothing. Her childless condition, like Mr Bonsor's, emerges from and exemplifies her passionless disposition. The suppression of Paul's youthful exuberance, inherited from his natural mother, the first Mrs Doubleday, is a logical consequence.

Paul is repeatedly imaged as a soldier, a warrior in the cause of freedom from cant and social hypocrisy. His triumph, which is the climax of the play, consists in a victory over the brutality of personal egotism. The weapons he employs are overt defiance and rededication to the Ibsenic ideal of self-realisation: like Nora Helmer and Dina Dorf he physically breaks out. Blanche Amber, at one point, urges him to yield fearlessly to his passions and uncompromising self-honesty; Nina Freshville, at another, echoing perhaps Martha Bernick's exhortation to Dina, encourages him to grasp life with both hands. By the third act he has come to realise that he is "as good as—as good as—well, as good as most men." This is not a satirical revelation along the lines of *Cosi Fan Tutte*. It is a personal discovery which, once made, completes his modulation towards self-fulfilment. He becomes entirely self-reconciled and, having assumed his rightful inheritance and position of authority in the family, breaks its claustrophobic hold.

This is a pattern repeated frequently in Ibsen: we might describe it as his dominant concern. In a letter to Gaspari in June, 1883, for example, he flatly denied the existence of any moral absolute save the obligation "to realise myself in spirit and in truth." In his plays he constantly circled the problem, counterposing the individual's dedication to this ideal against the consequences for society and himself. Occasionally, as in *Hedda Gabler* or *The Wild Duck*, the central figure realises either the wrong self or his real self in the wrong way; but more frequently Ibsen's injunction to his heroes and heroines—Brand, Lona Hessel, Dr Stockmann, Nora Helmer, Oswald and Helen Alving, Ellida Wangel, Johannes Rosmer and Rebecca West—is to pursue relentlessly the ideal of self-realisation in spirit and in truth.

In two of his earlier prose tragedies in particular, *A Doll's House* and *The Pillars of Society* (both of which we know James had studied in great detail), this problem is examined at great length. In both dramas, as Herman Weigand pointed out, passion or instinct is vindicated each time it finds itself in conflict with convention. Further, smugness and hypocrisy are castigated whenever they are present. Nora, crushed at first and, like Paul, without an

48

independent entity, breaks the bonds of her marriage in a single act of social defiance. This is imaged in the slamming of the Helmers' front door, just as Paul's revolt is imaged in his abrupt departure for London. Dina Dorf, in her stifled existence and final defiance, follows an evolution of thought and action which is strikingly similar. Assumed by her adoptive family to have somehow, like Paul, inherited her mother's deplorable proclivities, she acquiesces, at first, both in the patronising moral contempt in which she is held and in the harsh terms of her suppressed existence. She is filled with despair and self-disgust, and longs to break away to another place where passion will be recognised as natural and clean. In the meantime she keeps the rest of her world at bay:

> Then I must tell you that I'm not like other girls here; there's something—something about me. That's why you mustn't walk with me.

Paul also believes himself to belong to the Lapsed and Lost. In a similar speech he keeps the rest of his world at bay:

> I'm not like the others—I'm so easily upset! . . . My propensities, you know.

Finally, transformed by a personal crisis which contains clear parallels with Paul's, Dina defies the authority of the community and runs away with Johan Tönnessen. This release not only images the liberation of truth and freedom—the twin social pillars—but springs from that liberation itself. Dina's self-fulfilment becomes part of Bernick's: like Paul, Dina freed or enslaved is a symbol of the passionate commitment to life. Weigand comments about *The Pillars of Society*:

> Society as at present constituted is built on a foundation of sham and lies—that is the main thesis running through the play. But in intimate connection with the first, a second thesis is developed, namely that it is a society of bachelors, a man-made world, ruled by male egotism, assigning to women a position of subserviency and allowing no room for a woman to develop an independent personality of her own. This situation cries for revolution. We have here that trend of Ibsen's thought which reached its climax in his next two dramas, *A Doll's House* and *Ghosts*.

The society of *The Reprobate*, of which Paul's family is a faithful microcosm, is equally constituted of liars and deceivers, like Captain Chanter, who painfully hide their skeletons in closets worthy of the worst of Ibsen's haunted figures. James touches on the second thesis as well, only reversing the sexual struggle— the source of the comedy—so that it becomes the male ego that is repressed in a female-dominated world. Paul is not the only reprobate, nor is he the only prisoner. It is a situation which in its own way cries out for revolution, and James provides it. The play tells the story of Paul's revolt.

Jacques Barzun once argued, with some justification as I have tried to show, that *The Reprobate* is a grossly underrated play. Despite its rather pale humour and relative weakness when placed in the context of James's corpus as a whole, however, it nevertheless represents one of the real turning-points in his creative evolution. There is thus one further aspect of its achievement which must be discussed before we can go on to a consideration of James's later fiction: its remarkably complex structuring of image and symbol. This innovation, for it was no less, was subsequently to become an overwhelming factor in James's narrative prose.

The most striking aspect of the interplay between image and symbol in *The Reprobate* is the fact that it occurs at all. Never before in a drama had James attempted to exploit the possibilities thus offered. He had of course made some use of image and some use of symbol in his earlier fiction but, until his encounter with Ibsen, he had considered the stage too frivolous a medium to warrant the careful structuring which effective imagery required. Its introduction in a complex and intricate form into *The Reprobate* therefore suggests to my mind that he had ceased to think in terms of theatrical sows' ears and was considering more and more the production of silk purses. And there is a further important point. The use to which James put his images and symbols in this drama, and the manner in which he integrated them with each other and the overall meaning, constituted a radical departure in his work *as a whole*. I shall argue that he had never used imagery and symbolism in quite this way before and that, furthermore, it is a technical innovation strangely pre-echoed in Ibsen's work. It is in the movement from verbal image to physical symbol actualised on stage and integrated with the action at its deepest and shallowest levels that, I shall suggest, Ibsen's influence was most revolutionary and most profound. We may eventually come to feel that not only the form but the very substance of James's symbolism, in this drama and in his subsequent fiction, derived ultimately from Ibsen.

There are two major and recurring images in *The Reprobate*: water as an image of vitality, and physical sickness as an image of corruption. Although I shall be discussing primarily the former, both are carefully integrated with the symbol structure in the manner I have already indicated. It will be part of my argument, supporting the case for artistic derivation made above, that the first, the water imagery, was borrowed, consciously or otherwise, from *The Pillars of Society*. The second appears to be related to a similar set of ideas in *A Doll's House*. The broad point is that every aspect of James's imagery in this drama suggests that he had Ibsen strongly in mind when he wrote it.

Ibsen begins with a conventional metaphor in *The Pillars of Society*. Life is a wild and tossing sea; the community is a safe and protective port which shelters the ship of humanity and prepares it for the voyage of life. Moral honesty is the hull. If this is rotten when the human ship puts out, it will sink straight to the bottom. Ibsen makes his initial metaphor quite explicit:

> Rörlund: . . . What do *you* say, Miss Bernick? Do you not find that you have, as it were, firmer ground under your feet since you have given up your life to your school-work?
> Martha: I scarcely know what to say. Often when I am in the school-room I wish I were far out on the stormy sea.
> Rörlund: Yes, yes; that is the temptation, my dear Miss Bernick. You must bar the door against such an unquiet guest. The stormy sea—of course you do not mean that literally; you mean the great billowing world, where so many are wrecked . . .

Rörlund immediately begins to develop the metaphor, contrasting the land-bound community and its safety with the insecurity and dangers of the outside world-sea. He identifies security with those who live inland, indoors, like themselves. Later, literal references to the sea and its imaged or symbolic function become rapidly interwoven with the theme and plot of the whole play. The movement from simile (life is like the sea) to actuality exploited as symbol (*The Palm Tree* and *The Indian Girl*, Aune as shipwright and Bernick as the owner of a shipyard) to action integrated with the plot and deriving power from the verbal and symbolic context (Johan and Dina putting to sea in *The Indian Girl*, Olaf dabbling and fishing in the waters of the port and eventually stowing-away aboard a ship skimpily repaired in his father's shipyards), is deliberately and carefully thought out. Image, symbol and action are consistent with one another throughout the play. The sea is, or stands for, and in the end actually becomes, natural spontaneous real life. It is "real" in the sense that it stands in opposition to the stagnant, stale, hypocritical backwater within which Bernick and his family have enclosed themselves. Bernick acknowledges the further extension of the metaphor—that the community is a fleet of ships, a convoy in which each individual is his own vessel—when in the fourth act he admits, "There are many among us that need thorough and upright repairs."

In the series of oppositions which make up the structure of tension in *The Pillars of Society* it is the conflict between the values associated with the wild sea of the outside world and those of the sheltered harbour backwater of the little port which is the sharpest and most emphatically presented. These two correlatives pull into themselves, and unite into conflicting forces, the tense opposing elements in the play. This is no Hegelian conflict, however, in the sense that antithetical goods are involved, although a qualitatively superior synthesis emerges. For where "real life" involves freedom from stultifying convention and individual repression, and where the sea-life provides honesty in morality and natural behaviour, the backwater life festers in corruption, dishonesty, hypocrisy, selfishness; the individual chokes, stifles, suffers, and his pain is glossed over with cant or rationalisation or appeal to prejudice. The backwater life imposes its own regimen: on no account must its members come into contact with life proper, with the sea-life. Thus women are intimidated when they seek or ask about it (Martha and Betty); children are punished when they experiment with it (Olaf); and most adult men lack the courage to engage with it (Hilmer and Rörlund). We have, for example, already seen how Martha is quickly reproved by the Pastor for even toying vaguely with her desire for the life of the sea. When Olaf, whose fascination with the ocean is imaged in his persistent trips to the pier to fish, dips too deeply into life for Bernick's comfort, he is thrashed savagely. Even Hilmer, who once had a youthful vision of a life of adventure away from Norway, has become far too timid to follow through the logic of his aspirations. When confronted with the faintest possibility that his ideals might actually be realised, he either backs away timidly (as he does before the threat of Olaf's toy bow) or throws his hands up with a cry of disgust. Intimidated and frightened, he is the pathetic idealist.

The sea-life, therefore, has Ibsen's full approval. When Johan and Dina fall in love and run away, their union is symbolised in their "putting to sea" together. It is at this point—the embarkation of the boats—that verbal image and symbol and metaphor coalesce most strikingly with the action. Image, symbol and action have become fully integrated; metaphor has become intrinsic.

The image/symbol nexus in *The Reprobate* recalls this process to a remarkable degree. It is founded, as in *The Pillars of Society*, on an extended water metaphor. From it, as I have already suggested, a series of images and symbols grow which are gradually integrated with the action in the manner we have just been discussing. Pitt Brunt, for example, the hesitant M.P. for Blackport, whose quietly respectable passion for Blanche so resembles Rörlund's for Dina, enters during the opening minutes wearing "a modified boating suit"—he has just come off the river. In this minor stage direction James displays how completely he had understood (and borrowed) Ibsen's idea. Brunt, who is "very neat, and deliberate and slightly hesitant", ventures on to the river in a suit only modified for the occasion: his contact with life is characteristically restrained, slightly distasteful. His commitment is never full-blooded. On the other hand, Nina Freshville, a character whose actions and attitudes seem to me profoundly shaped by Ibsen's Lona Hessel, is his direct polar opposite. Their contrasting attitudes to life are played off against each other just as are Rörlund's and Lona's. Brunt regularly puts in his dutiful hour on the river each day as part of a considered routine; Nina by contrast tells us that during her youth she would spend hours on the stream simply for the pleasure it afforded. Thus right from the opening moments James's play follows Ibsen's. A character's attitude to water indicates his attitude to life; for water is life itself. The deliberate counter-balancing of Brunt's and Nina's attitudes towards the river initiates the gradual integration of image and action which is to run consistently through the play. In the final act, as in *The Pillars of Society*, James spells out his metaphor. Brunt, who has continued to court Blanche right to the end, encounters her as he is on his way to put in his daily hour. He immediately invites her to join him. In terms of the play's imagery this reflects Brunt's larger proposal, that she should marry him and accompany him through life. Blanche refuses both invitations when she replies, "Ah, your boat's not my boat, and it's impossible for me to embark with you!" Having struck this ambiguous note, prepared for it as it were, James brings the analogic meaning fully out into the open when Brunt retorts, "I want you to embark, you know, on the river of life; to float with me down the crystal stream." Blanche takes up the image and draws all its conclusions to a point. She refuses Brunt because his "crystal stream of life . . . flows into the Smutt at Blackport. I don't find that a tempting voyage." As Blanche exits Brunt laments ambiguously, "She won't come out with me in the boat." This is clearly a Jamesian stress—one might almost say over-stress —that the metaphor is to be taken seriously. Later Mr Bonsor, who is anxious that Blanche marry Brunt, threatens to "carry her on board" himself.

James subsequently exploits the water imagery in terms of his central thematic concern. Paul's public defiance and abrupt departure for London initiates a discussion about his ethics and contact with life which is expressed in an amazing sequence of water images, an extended metaphorical exercise, which reflects both forwards and backwards through the play. Chanter has been sent in hot pursuit, a mission of retrieval; and after searching unsuccessfully for Paul he sends a telegram which arrives just after Blanche's last exit. Its wording is both an extension of and a deliberate reference to the imagery that has just been used and carefully explained: "Last hope dashed—evidently sunk to the bottom." Paul, in breaking the moral and physical bounds of his family, has sunk himself in life. Mrs Doubleday, taking up the metaphor, immediately fears that he has sunk "lower than any sounding", an image which recalls her earlier vision of him, in the first act, "steeped to the lips" in vice. Mr Bonsor replies that, in order to retrieve Paul, Chanter will require "the equipment of a diver", wrongly assuming that vice is not Chanter's natural habitat.

Like the Bernick household the Doubleday's is made up of land animals who fear the sea. They require special equipment when coming into contact with the passionate existence of the waters. They are themselves without passion; by definition anti-life, stultified by duty, high and dry. What is being counterposed against "real" life in this drama is bourgeois morality: as in Norway, so in England. The antithesis is of course in a sense a real one, though we have here the unexpected situation of none other than Henry James—so committed, as we have seen, to flattering the prejudices of his middle-class audiences—offering a critique of the conventional posture by holding it up to ridicule. It marks an important departure in his attitude towards the theatre public.

Mr Bonsor, continuing his discussion with Mrs Doubleday, promises her that after Paul has been recovered from the depths he will have to be "pumped dry", though she fears that he "would *never* be dry!" Bonsor continues:

> We should doubtless have more than ever, in our intercourse with him, to make use of the moral mackintosh.
>
> Mrs Doubleday: I impressed upon Captain Chanter from the first the necessity for such a garment.

The opposed values and their associated symbols are quite clear. And they are exactly the same as in *The Pillars of Society*. Morality, duty, bourgeois conventionality are safe and dry; the land is the area in which they are to be found. But passion, action, youthful exuberant vitality, are wet, dangerous, to be kept at bay by the moral mackintosh or appropriate diving gear. Better still, by not swimming at all. Or if you must go into the river go in a boat, do it in moderation and, above all, don't enjoy yourself.

The intense sequence of water images in this last act high-lights an earlier series. In the first act Chanter had referred to that passion which, long repressed, "bursts forth in a flood", and a little later Mrs Doubleday, not taking up the Captain's image, but constructing one of her own, describes how Paul's vile morals, inherited from his mother in the Ibsenesque fashion already discussed, were repressed "until his twentieth year. Then they burst forth." His mother was like a fountain, pouring forth corruption;

it was not until her death that the "fatal fountain . . . ceased to flow". Finally, in the concluding sequences in the play, when the apposite couples are paired off ("the time-honoured bread sauce of the happy ending"), the event is imaged in terms of the prevailing symbolism. Paul induces Nina to accept Brunt and she indicates her agreement by literally joining him in his boat on the river. This not only looks back to the exchange between Brunt and Blanche but immediately recalls the final scene in *The Pillars of Society* when Dina and Johan put to sea together. Image and action have coalesced.

In this play, then, as it seems to me, James shows himself to have become a dramatist peculiarly sensitive to Ibsen's example. The whole ethos of his theatre work has altered—from that of the light-weight Scribean fantasy, the farce of manners (as in *The Album*), to that of the more serious, considered probings of the Ibsen drama. In this James was not alone; throughout the London theatre world contemporary British dramatists (Pinero and H. A. Jones to name two) were beginning to follow the Norwegian's lead. But of course, and the point must be stressed, James did not become an Ibsenist in his work overnight. *The Reprobate* remains a comedy, and a rather feeble one at that. Still, it embodies comedy of another kind, comedy touched with seriousness. Furthermore, as I think I have shown, it follows Ibsen in many important respects—the delineation of character, the treatment of situation as opposed to action, the exploitation of the possibilities of image and symbol. *The Reprobate*, granted, is not simply and not only a Jamesian version of (say) *The Pillars of Society* or *A Doll's House*—my argument, after all, is for influence, not plagiarism. Nevertheless it is clearly a play in which Ibsen's formative presence may be plainly detected.

2

Other Houses, Other Inks

It is not my intention to suggest that Ibsen's influence on James was all-pervasive in the sense of acting with equal intensity on everything he wrote after the crucial period when he began seriously to examine the Norwegian's plays. James was so complex a writer, so capable of constructing variegated forms, and so continuously experimentive, that to reduce his later work—and it would be a reduction—to a single impulse is patently absurd. Some pieces, especially the late tales dealing with the plight of the failed novelist, or the opportunity missed, or the long-awaited great event which never in fact arrives, are barely touched by Ibsen's hand at all. Indeed, they are so pointedly autobiographical —titles like *Embarrassments* and *Terminations*, published immediately after the theatre fiasco, cry out for comment of this sort— that many critics treat them as exercises in memoir or self-definition, along with *Notes of a Son and Brother*, the Prefaces, and *The American Scene*. But contrarily there are those pieces, usually novels or nouvelles ("long fictions with a complicated subject" as opposed to "concise anecdote", according to James himself) which quite clearly reveal themselves as profoundly affected by Ibsen. *The Other House*, which we will look at briefly in a moment, is a striking case in point.

What I have been able to establish so far in this book may tempt one to the conclusion that James's sudden interest in Ibsen may have led to a flurry of imitation in the early nineties in the hope of short-term theatrical gains, but that in the aftermath of dramatic disillusion Ibsen's influence, if present at all, became so diffuse as to be only a marginal and indistinguishable presence. I hope in the course of this chapter and the next to demonstrate the limitations of such a conclusion. During James's middle period, from *The Spoils of Poynton* to *The Awkward Age*, Ibsen continued to make himself crucially felt, and I shall try to establish this by examining what I take to be the high points. These include not only *The Other House* and *The Spoils of Poynton*, both conceived during 1893 as plays but executed during 1895–6 as novels, but also such apparently tangential works as *The Turn of the Screw* and its companion piece in *The Two Magics* (1898), *Covering End*. This last, in particular, appears to have exercised a peculiar fascination for its author. It was written initially as a play for Ellen Terry, was subsequently turned into a nouvelle some three years later, and was finally restructured as a three-act drama, *The High Bid*, during James's second theatre phase of 1907–9. Its history, so like that of *The Other House*, reveals James's continuing involvement with its form, its subject and its starkly Ibsenic emphases.

Throughout this period, then, Ibsen was a continuing presence at his elbow whenever he wrote extended, complicated, narrative prose fictions. He began with scenario, with scenic design; and then slipped quite naturally (sometimes more deeply than others) into drawing upon Ibsen's content. His work as a whole became more sombre, more severe and increasingly despairing; it is filled with an Ibsenesque sense of human infirmity and sometimes disgust. Sexual corruption and frustration is a recurring theme, presented repeatedly in conflict and contrast with the innocence of children—Maisie, Nanda, Miles and Flora, Effie Bream. They are the ones who suffer, the victims of a degenerate world. At this time, the period of his rededication to the novelist's art, the period when, with mounting excitement he was trying to integrate the gains of his dramatic years with his skills as a narrator, he moved away sharply from the simpler antitheses of America and Europe which characterised his earlier fiction, to a more profound and self-conscious investigation of the hypocrisies of Victorian England, finding within that society itself sufficient antitheses to support his evolving moral vision. The violation of childish innocence, so characteristic of the plays which Ibsen was producing at this time, and which James was handsomely defending in the press, found its way increasingly into his own work. Without wishing to argue too strongly for direct influence at this point—but claiming everything for indirection—I might venture that the often tragic situations in which James's children find themselves in the novels of this period owe at least something—occasionally, as in *The Other House*, a striking parallel—to the pressure wrought by such productions as *The Wild Duck* and *Little Eyolf*. Of this last play, in particular, James was almost excessive in his praise when he first read it—one of those moments of almost manic submission to the power of Ibsen's drama which contrast so strangely with the bitterness of his hostility elsewhere. When in 1894 the publisher William Heinemann sent him a proof copy of the first two acts of the play James replied:

> I feel as if I couldn't thank you enough for introducing me to Ibsen's prodigious little performance! I return it to you, by the same post conscientiously after two breathless perusals, which leave me with a yearning as impatient, an appetite as hungry, for the rest, as poor Rita's yearning and appetite are for the missing caresses of her Alfred. Do satisfy me better or more promptly than he satisfied her. The thing is immensely characteristic and immensely—immense. I quite agree with you that it takes hold as nothing else of his has as yet done—it appeals with an immoderate intensity, and goes straight as a dose of castor oil! . . . If he really carries on the whole play with these four people—and at the same high pitch (its the *pitch* that's so magnificent) it will be a feat more extraordinary than any he's achieved—it will beat *Ghosts*. Admirable, gallant old man!

In his review of the play's première in London three years later James was equally enthusiastic. Ibsen's genius rivalled Shakespeare's—indeed, for his part, said James, he preferred Ibsen. *Little Eyolf* was as fine a production as *Richard III*, and he went on to acknowledge his "acceptance of the small Ibsen *spell*, the surrender of the imagination to his microcosm, his confined but completely constituted world, in which, in every case, the tissue of relations between the parts and the whole is of a closeness so fascinating."

The Other House was Henry James's first full-blown Ibsen tragedy. This point has been made so often and so eloquently by many excellent critics—see, for example, Leon Edel's Introduction to the 1948 edition of the novel—that it would be wasteful and repetitious to dwell for long upon it here. The point, I think, would be granted by most. In this novel, conceived, it will be remembered, first as a play in 1893, Ibsen vanquished Scribe forever. Even *Guy Domville*, composed at approximately the same time, was marred by James's attempt to somehow integrate the gains of the Scribean play with the highly Ibsenesque situation which forms the basis of the action. It could well be argued that Guy, the saint caught between the demands of his lineage and the promptings of his convictions, is a figure modelled to some extent on Rosmer of Rosmersholm. Contemporary critics like Shaw and Wells immediately detected the unevenness in quality when, in the second act, James reverted to a French example to further the action. Especially disastrous was his attempt to imitate the drinking scene from Augier's *L'Aventurière*. But where James stuck to Ibsen, as in the first and third acts, he clearly impressed at least part of his audience.

The Other House, however, is pure Ibsen, unalloyed, undistilled and hawked directly from the pages of *Hedda Gabler* and *Rosmersholm*. Briefly, it tells the story of Rose Armiger, Hedda Gabler in a Jamesian hat, who drowns a little girl, Effie Bream, in order to free herself of a sexual rival, Jean Martle, by casting suspicion for the murder on her. The triangle of tensions which produces the violence and conflicts in this play-novel (an "extended prompt-book" as James thought of it) is an almost exact copy of the triangular arrangement underlying the tragedy of *Hedda Gabler*. In Ibsen's play the major tensions spring from the struggle between Hedda and Thea for Eilert Lövberg; in *The Other House* they arise from a similar tussle between Rose and Jean for Tony Bream, the child's father. Just as Thea is almost unaware of the struggle, her innocence perhaps being her most potent weapon, so Jean is almost wholly ignorant of the battle or the cause for which she is fighting. She has only her innocent love for Tony. Against both these sweet, rather vapid but deeply-feminine young women is pitted all the selfish intelligence of a malicious, neurotic, beautiful woman, capable of beguiling and outwitting everyone around her. Both Rose and Hedda are motivated by the same passionate idealisation of their men, and both are ruthless in achieving their desires.

Yet this is where their affinities begin, not end. Rose Armiger is a gifted, handsome woman, as I have said; yet her life is barren. Like Hedda Gabler, destructive will-power is the key to her personality and the secret of the fascination she exerts, for the tension between passionate aspiration and frustrated consummation is her characteristic mode. She wills, and is denied. To the bald, provincial world of *The Other House* she presents a cool, detached exterior; but within she rages. From time to time, when she is alone, her face convulses "strangely, tragically", as if she is suppressing "with extraordinary force some passionate sob or cry, some smothered impulse or anguish". Yet when she is interrupted she turns upon her visitor with a smile and makes light conversation. Rose's control is tight; as tight as Hedda Gabler's. The passage I have just cited recalls in detail Hedda's despair in Act I when Ibsen directs: "she walks about the room raising her arms and clenching her hands in desperation. Then she flings back the glass door, and stands there looking out." Presently Tesman returns and Hedda utters some banality to him, "once more calm and mistress of herself."

It is this moment, and others like it, which illustrates the anguish, the suffering and the pathetic humanity which James, in his own analysis of the play, felt to be her distinguishing trait:

> She suffers, she struggles, she is human, and by that fact exposed to a dozen interpretations, to the importunity of our suspense.

Clearly James has worked this quality of ambiguous tension quite consciously into his own struggling, suffering heroine. After the murder Rose is unable to explain her grotesque, mad action except in terms of a wild, uncontrollable impulse which smashed through her defences like a storm. Her inner tension broke out, expressing itself in a malevolent gesture of hatred, defiance and insanity. "It was all that I saw—it was all that possessed me. It took hold of me, it possessed me: it was the last gleam of a chance . . . It's a storm that's past, it's a debt that's paid." In this speech she owes more, perhaps, to Rebecca West than Hedda Gabler. Explaining the motives which led her to drive Beata to suicide Rebecca confesses: "It came upon me like a storm on the sea. It was like one of those storms we sometimes have in the North in the winter-time. It seizes you—and sweeps you along with it—whither it will. Resistance is out of the question." Hedda is also swept along by uncontrollable passions. She admits: "Well, you see—these impulses come over me all of a sudden; and I *cannot* resist them. Oh, I don't know how to explain it."

James's perception of this strange, destructive quality in Hedda leads straight to Rose's irrational, almost pathological malignancy. Both she and Hedda are impelled by motives which have no rational base; they are passions only. James wrote of Hedda:

> Her motives are just her passions. What the four acts show us is these motives and that character—complicated, strange, irreconcilable, infernal—playing themselves out.

What the three Books of *The Other House* show us are these same, or similar, passions in Rose Armiger playing themselves out in a Jamesian world virtually indistinguishable from Ibsen's. Like Hedda her personality is strange, complicated, irreconcilable, infernal—an almost exact copy. Yet what struck James most about Ibsen's complex heroine was precisely her heroic stature; her ambiguity; the trick of personality that rendered her both seductive and repulsive. He wrote of her:

> And then one isn't sure she is wicked, and by no means sure (especially when she is represented by an actress who makes the point ambiguous) that she is disagreeable. She is various and sinuous and graceful, complicated and natural.

James might have been writing of Rose Armiger, so accurately do these words describe her. When a couple of years after writing these lines he began to compose *The Promise*, the original title for *The Other House*, he took as his central figure a personality as deliberately ambiguous as Hedda, a woman "infinitely perverse . . . a perfectly ill-regulated person", who baffles everyone around her with her complex perversity and strange ambiguity. Indeed, ambiguity is the essence, not only of Rose's personality, but of any response to it. James goes to some lengths to stress both things. Rose lies, cheats, dissembles, then immediately contradicts herself with stunning candour. She is made to "murmur" things "ambiguously", permitting half-inferences to be drawn from even her most casual remarks. Thus quite like Hedda she is exposed to a dozen interpretations, and all are indulged in at some point. Her elusiveness is part of her fascination.

The argument is clinched, I think, if we compare the acts of destructive jealousy which Rose and Hedda commit—the burning of Eilert's manuscript and the murder of Tony's child. It will also serve to answer Oscar Cargill's lonely objection that James cannot have had *Hedda Gabler* in mind when constructing his tragedy because in Ibsen's play "there is no murdered child." As I shall show, however, the infanticide theme is one of the most powerful links in the chain connecting the two dramas.

Why does Rose murder Effie? We cannot tell. She is insane, jealous, swept along by passions unknown, half-capable of articulating a motive (to throw the blame on Jean) yet muttering, as she carries the child to her doom, "It's as your dear, dead mother's, my own sweet, that—if it's time—I shall carry you to bed!" The parenthetical phrase, "if it's time", suggests the years of hidden jealousy. She kills because the child stands between her and Tony; because it is the product of his union with her schoolfriend Julia; because its care has become the way in which Jean expresses her love for its father. She takes the little girl to the water, plunges her into it, makes sure she is dead and then walks coldly back to the house. It is an act of calm deliberation built on a foundation of seething emotion. Yet the fact of her deed displays her emotional sterility.

The scene of Effie's murder recalls *Rosmersholm*; but the act itself comes straight out of *Hedda Gabler*. Why does Hedda burn Eilert's manuscript? Again, we cannot fully tell. Her passions, like Rose's, are complex, contradictory, half-perceived and almost pathological. Yet near to the core is a most terrible, yearning jealousy of Thea Elvsted's fecundity. As she feeds the manuscript page by page into the flames she whispers to herself, "Now I am burning your child, Thea! Your child and Eilert Lövborg's. I am burning—I am burning your child." Ibsen is quite unequivocal about this point. He repeatedly stresses the infanticide theme throughout the play:

> Mrs Elvsted: Do you know, Lövborg, that what you've done with the book—I shall think of it to my dying day as though you had killed a child.
> Lövborg: Yes, you are right. It's like a sort of child-murder.
> Mrs Elvsted: How could you then—! Did not the child belong to me too?
> Hedda: [almost inaudibly] Ah, the child—

And later, when Brack is describing to Hedda the real circumstances of Eilert's death: "He was there this afternoon. He came to claim something, he said, which they had taken from him. Talked wildly about a lost child . . ."

There is no need, I think, to labour the point further. *The Other House*, like *The Reprobate*, is the portrait of a nature, of a state of nerves and of soul, of chagrin and despair. Interest focuses on Rose and her complex, intriguing, intricate personality; and everything comes to a climax when, as in *Hedda Gabler*, the "bad heroine" (the phrase James coined for Rose) commits a brutal crime. Both are literary first cousins.

There are two last points to be made about James's play-novel. First, Rose—unlike Hedda in this regard—does not commit suicide when she is finally discovered. Her doom, as Tony says, will be to live with herself in the years to come. Why James departed from *Hedda Gabler* at this point we cannot say precisely. In his review of the play, however, he did remark that, to his mind, Hedda's suicide blurs her type-quality, smudges the complexity of her personality and edges the play towards a description of madness entire. The suicide detracts from the moral complexity of her situation. After stressing his insight that Ibsen tends to deal with the individual "caught in the fact" James observes:

> Sometimes, no doubt, he leans too far on that side, loses sight too much of the type-quality and gives his spectators free play to say that even caught in the fact his individuals are mad. We are not at all sure, for instance, of the type-quality in Hedda.

Brack's response to Hedda's suicide—"people don't *do* such things!"—is of course an anticipation by Ibsen of this sort of critique; he eliminates your objection by providing it himself. James may have decided, however, in his own version of the play, to keep the issues clear. He presents us instead, without an ending that may have looked too much like melodrama or cheap plagiarism, with a formidable study of an exasperated personality caught in a difficult and morally complex fact.

The second important departure from *Hedda Gabler* in *The Other House* is the novel's Prologue—what became the first act of the play when it was written some ten years later. In it James sketches in the background to Rose's deed, and gives something of the history of her passion. He gives us an introductory act, as it were, in which Rosmer and Rebecca hover about the bed of the dying Beata—an act which culminates in Beata's suicide. Or, to take the alternative example, James creates a first act in which the reasons for Hedda's violent and perplexing behaviour are given a context and a history; he shows us Hedda, so to speak, attracted to Lövborg but afraid of her passion, whispering with him over her illustrated newspapers while the General snores away left-of-centre. At the end of the act she panics and marries Tesman.

Again, James's review of *Hedda Gabler* provides a helpful clue, since it was the absence of just such a Prologue as this which he felt to be the only real defect in the play. One could doubtless imagine other ways, he observed gnomically, of approaching its subject matter; yet

> Something might have been gained, entailing perhaps a loss in another direction, by tracing the preliminary stages, showing the steps in Mrs Tesman's history which led to the spasm, as it were, on which the curtain rises and of which the breathless duration—ending in death—is the period of the piece . . . We receive Hedda ripe for her catastrophe, and if we ask for antecedents and explanations we must simply find them in her character.

It is reasonable to suppose, therefore, that James decided to follow his own advice—and to gain something, perhaps?—when he sat down to work on his own approach to the study of an exasperated woman modelled closely on Hedda Gabler. When *The Other House* opens Julia Bream, though still alive, is dying in childbirth. The major characters, Rose, Tony, Jean and Dennis Vidal—the Tesman-like figure who wants to marry Rose—are introduced and carefully described. In particular, the bewildering tensions of Rose's strange personality, providing some basis for an understanding of her future violence, are indicated and tautened. The Second Book, which is thus effectively the first act of the play, begins exactly four years later with the accidental and coincidental meeting of all the major figures at the same place, the house at Wilverley, and at the same time, Effie Bream's birthday. Two central events in the Prologue create the complex, morally intricate situation which dominates the rest of the story: Julia Bream's death, and the revelation of Tony's promise to her (never to inflict a stepmother on Effie). A context and a history for the rest of the tragedy is thus provided.

The Other House was drawn up during 1893 in a period when James's mind was saturated with Ibsen. Elizabeth Robins records in *Theatre and Friendship* how he would visit her almost daily during the winter of 1892-3 to have Ibsen's new play, *The Master Builder,* translated for him while the ink was still wet, so to speak, on the printer's galleys. Too impatient to wait for the forthcoming Archer-Gosse translation, James joined the select band of people who were allowed to see Miss Robins's copy of the Norwegian text.

Throughout the London literary world the news of Ibsen's new play was causing the greatest excitement. The controversy had subsided somewhat during 1892; now each side prepared itself for fresh encounters in the press and in the theatre. The play arrived piecemeal, act by act, in "violently agitating spurts—or as one might say, in volts, projected across the North Sea in a series of electric shocks", as Elizabeth Robins puts it. She goes on:

> The news of their arrival flew from the Strand to Manchester Square Gardens, from there to Yorkshire and to De Vere Gardens [where James was living]—while I sat and hugged my good luck in being able to read the Norwegian . . . Mr James, being in London, could come himself and so hear more than I had time to write.

It was also during this period that James, one gathers, made a small but obviously significant attempt to learn Norwegian—presumably the better to read Ibsen. He bought a grammar, at any rate, but after poring over it for a while wryly sent it on to his translator. Her freely-given services in this regard were adequate for his needs though, as his attempt to learn the language showed, he was determined to come to grips with Ibsen as fully as possible. His letters to Miss Robins are filled with references to "the great news" and the intense "eagerness" with which he looked forward to her renderings. A typical passage is the following, taken from a letter he wrote her a few days before a translating session. We can gather from it that they had already read about half the first act together, and had stopped just before the entrance of Hilda Wangel. James's speculations as to which of the drama's three women was eventually to emerge as the heroine relate largely to Miss Robins's hope that the new play would provide a suitable vehicle for her talents, and indeed she eventually played Hilda when it opened in London a few months later:

> It is all painfully, terribly interesting! I am fully impatient for Tuesday afternoon—and beside myself with curiosity as to who or

what the "other woman" can be. *This* reflection—however—is somewhat lurid—that Kaia, the black-silk wife, another woman *must* be (in a 3-act play and by the middle of the 1st) the *only* woman, so that the "heroine" is, of necessity, one or other of them. Perhaps she *is* the black-silk wife. You don't tell me whether the other woman is the wife of the "young couple." Nor whether the thunder roll from the *other* translator (on receipt of emendations) has yet come back to you. These things, however, I must curb myself to wait for till Tuesday at 5.

What makes this extract particularly interesting is its concern with the technical details of Ibsen's first act, apart from the speculations about the heroine. James was never merely a passive admirer of Ibsen. When *The Master Builder* finally went into production in February, 1893, he attended not only rehearsals but almost every performance—and Archer records that thirty in all were given. On February 21 he wrote to Miss Robins, "I shan't see the *M.B.* again today, but I expect tomorrow, or at the furthest Thursday."

A few days before this, on February 17, the *Pall Mall Gazette* published his second public statement on Ibsen. Ostensibly concerned with the new production—it was headed "Ibsen's New Play"—this piece completes the analysis he had begun nearly two years earlier. As we have noted, he in fact published the two together as a single chapter in his *Essays in London and Elsewhere* later in the year.

James begins by recapitulating the main points in his first piece: Ibsen deals characteristically with "the supremely critical hour in the life of an individual, in the history of a soul"; he makes his work breathe with "the sense of life" and so forth. In passing he acknowledges, significantly we may feel, the "inward strife which is an inevitable heritage of all inquiring contact with the master", and he accepts "the hard compulsion of his strangely inscrutable art" with its uncanny ability to weave "a more or less irritating spell" which commands submission—subjection is the word James actually uses. But then he goes on to a fresh insight. Ibsen is not just the dramatist of crises; he is a symbolist—and we see James moving here from evaluation to analysis—whose technique involves the close interrelation between literal action ("the reality") and the controlling metaphysic ("the idea"). Ibsen's symbolism reinforces the effect and intention of the whole in any of his dramas (but particularly in *The Master Builder*); reality and symbol are intermingled.

> The mingled reality and symbolism of it all gives us an Ibsen within an Ibsen. His subject is always, like the subjects of all first-rate men, primarily an idea; but in this case [*The Master Builder*] the idea is as difficult to catch as its presence is impossible to over-look. The whole thing throbs and flushes with it, and yet smiles and mocks at us through it as if in conscious supersubtlety.

James is fully aware that while the play cannot be reduced satisfactorily to its surface action—the final crisis in the life of Solness—allegory, on the other hand, is not Ibsen's intention. The solution lies between, on some artistic plane where action and symbol meet to create a total experience. There is a symbiosis be-tween the facts of the action and the details of the controlling symbolism which in conjunction yield "the vivified whole."

> The action at any rate is superficially simple, more single and confined than that of most of Ibsen's other plays; practically, as it defines itself and rises to a height, it leaves the strange doomed Solness, and the even stranger apparition of the joyous and impor-tunate girl (the one all memories and hauntings and bondages, the other all health and curiosity and youthful insolence), face to face on unprecedented terms . . .

The acuteness of James's analysis, for all its baffled admiration, is outstanding when we compare it with most of the criticism of his contemporaries. Many thought Ibsen simply a lunatic; others, like Archer and Gosse, took the play to be an autobiographic alle-gory. When neither explanation was seen to account sufficiently for the play's power, easy parallels with Maeterlinck were drawn: *The Master Builder* and *The Blue Bird* were of the same genre, idealist constructs in which every detail (like Mrs Solness's nine dolls) bore strange symbolic relevance to the prevailing trans-cendentalism. Viewed in this way *The Master Builder* provoked even further controversy when these same details stubbornly refused to fit a broader hypothesis.

What James understood, however, was that the symbolism of Ibsen's later period was only partly related in spirit and technique to the reaction which came to be known as *symbolisme* in France in the 1880s. Ibsen's commitment to the spare and the real, which

James found so attractive, was the antithesis of a movement whose leaders were concerned, as Jean Leymarie once put it, "no longer with an objective picture of the outer world, but with the fantastic imagery of their dreams, luxuriantly dressed up in symbolic and decorative trappings." What distinguishes *symbolisme* from Ibsenism is its commitment to an essentially incommunicable individual experience expressed analogically through an esoteric stream of images unique to the individual himself. The anti-Realist and, as Edmund Wilson would have it, late Romantic spirit of the movement, is defined by him as "an attempt by carefully studied means—a complicated association of ideas represented by a medley of metaphors—to communicate unique personal feelings." He adds elsewhere in *Axel's Castle*:

> But the symbols of the Symbolist school are usually chosen arbitrarily by the poet to stand for special ideas of his own— they are a sort of disguise for these ideas. "The Parnassians for their part", wrote Mallarmé, "take the thing just as it is and put it before us—and consequently they are deficient in mystery: they deprive the mind of the delicious joy of believing that it is creating. To name an object is to do away with the three-quarters of the enjoyment of the poem which is derived from the satisfaction of guessing little by little: to suggest it, to evoke it—that is what charms the imagination."

What Ibsen was trying to do in his final period, however, was something quite different: the interaction of "reality" and "idea" through the extension of metaphor. James showed how this process is illustrated in *The Master Builder* when he described Hilda as the "animated clock-face" of Halvard Solness's destiny, the "indirect form" of his fate. She is literally, metaphorically and symbolically youth hammering at his door to be be let in. *Symboliste* playwrights like Maeterlinck, and painters like Van Gogh and Gaugin, consciously avoided making the distinction between their symbols and the real world. As Bowra puts it, in Maeterlinck's drama "the characters have no personality but are symbols of the poet's dreams." Ibsen's artistry on the other hand lay in his ability to use symbols and images to reinforce the impact of his dramatic reality; to energise, in a word, the banal setting of the drawing-room play.

What I shall suggest in later chapters is that James's grasp of this technique, and his profound admiration of it, led finally to its total assimilation in his own work. James's analysis anticipates his own late manner precisely: the interaction of "reality" and "idea" so that the whole throbs and flushes and yet smiles and mocks at us as if in conscious supersubtlety.

Covering End, the rather neglected nouvelle which was published together with *The Turn of the Screw* as the second of *The Two Magics* (written under the same Ibsen spell?) in 1898, is a study of *genius loci*, of the tangible spirit of a home, which is related directly in theme and preoccupation to *The Spoils of Poynton*. As Gorley Putt remarks, its theme is "a restatement in an innocent C-Major key of the discordant faith of Mrs Gereth." As we have already noted, it was written initially as a one-act play for Ellen Terry, *Summersoft*, in 1895; three years later it was turned into the nouvelle we now have (retaining fully its dramatic structure along extended prompt-book lines); and in 1907 it was recreated as a three-act drama, *The High Bid*, during James's second unsuccessful attempt to make a name for himself as a playwright.

Briefly, it tells the story of a home, Covering End, and the benign influence which it exerts on a dedicated radical who has inherited it. Once again we have the portrait of a condition, the imitation not of an action—very little happens, save in the mind of the hero—but of a state of thought and tension.

Captain Yule, the radical in question, finds himself caught between the demands of his socialist conscience and the insistent Tory values of which his home is the abiding repository. At the end of the play he undergoes conversion to the new point of view—Covering End's—and marries its forceful and eloquent spokeswoman, Mrs Gracedew. The political debate which is the substance of James's tale thus resolves itself into a synthesis of the antithetical positions maintained throughout: Yule accepts his higher responsibilities—to Tradition and to the enduring, quasi-mystical values which transcend the petty quotidian realm of local politics—but in the name of a greater humanity. He abandons men in order to serve Man.

This theme has its affinities not only with *The Spoils of Poynton* (as I shall further argue) but, in an inverted way, with Ibsen's

Rosmersholm. James recreates for his hero the predicament confronting Rosmer in order to demonstrate, in his own play, the contrary conclusion. Both Yule and Rosmer are drawn into a political struggle where all the forces of modern society are mobilised to pressure their return to the traditionally conservative forces which are their heritage. Where Rosmer is confronted by the wily and self-seeking Kroll, Yule is faced with the equally cunning and opportunist Prodmore. Both these arch-reactionaries represent sectional interests eager to exploit for short-term political gain the prestige and reputation of, in Ibsen's play, Rosmer of Rosmersholm and, in James's nouvelle, Yule of Covering End. Both men endeavour without scruple to reverse the political apostasy of a Radical idealist whose name and family have for generations been traditionally associated with the Conservative interest. So prestigious are the names of Yule and Rosmer, and for so long have their families given a political lead to the county, that their public loyalties have become matters of crucial and decisive importance in the immediate political arena. Yule explains: "I'm the bearer of my name. I'm the representative of my family; and to my family and my name—since you've led me to it—the countryside has for generations been indulgently attached." Prodmore, like Kroll, is of course fully aware of this fact; his intention is to exploit it. He presents his appeal to Yule with some subtlety, however, arguing not from political expedience but from Duty and Tradition. Kroll argues in the same terms:

> . . . and to crown all, you have your venerable family name!
> Rosmer: Oh, my family name—
> Kroll: [points to the portraits] Rosmers of Rosmersholm—clergymen and soldiers; government officials of high place and trust; gentlemen to the fingertips, every man of them—a family that for nearly two centuries has held its first place in the district. Rosmer, you owe it to yourself and to the traditions of your race to take your share in guarding all that has hitherto been held sacred in our society.

Kroll argues from three directions: the political traditions of the Rosmers, the suggestion that they are a race apart—natural leaders of their community—and Rosmer's own heritage of duty to his inheritance. Prodmore appeals on the same terms to Yule. He urges him to return to the values of "the ancient cradle of

71

your race", gesturing as he does so to the family portraits hanging on the walls. When Yule doubts, as does Rosmer, whether he
can turn his political coat with honour Prodmore replies with a
speech which directly recalls Kroll's words above:

> "You'll only be turning it back again the way it was always worn.
> Gossage will receive you with open arms and press you to a heaving
> Tory bosom. That bosom"—Mr Prodmore followed himself up—
> "has never heaved but to sound Conservative principles. The cradle,
> as I've called it, or at least the rich, warm coverlet—of your race,
> Gossage was the political property, so to speak, of generations of
> your family. Stand therefore in the good old interest and you'll stand
> like a lion."

The resemblance between this and Kroll's appeal to Rosmer is
striking. James might have had Charles Archer's translation before
him when he wrote it.

The political struggles in *Rosmersholm* and *Covering End*, however, are only the backcloths to the moral—one might almost say
metaphysical—conflict which is at the centre of either work. They
are emblems, active examples, perhaps, of the violent collision
between absolute and relative values which is the real concern of
each. As James puts it, "it was as if two hard spirits, the grim
genius loci and the quick modern conscience, stood an instant
confronted." This comment, which could be applied equally to
Rosmersholm, points to the parallel antitheses in both plays. A
grim but enduring Past, expressed in the spirit of an ancient manor,
confronts the relativist reasoning of Victorian reformism. Where
Mrs. Gracedew pleads eloquently for History and the rich accre-
tions of tradition, Captain Yule retorts with an overwhelming case
for the greatest happiness of the greatest number. "I see something
else in the world than the beauty of old show-houses and the glory
of old show-families. There are thousands of people in England who
can show no houses at all, and I don't feel it utterly shameful to
share their poor fate!"

James unquestionably associates himself with this statement,
at least in part. Covering End itself is cold, crumbling and sterile;
as Yule comments, "The cradle of my race bears for me, Mr Prodmore, a striking resemblance to its tomb." James takes great care
to emphasise the manor's deathly qualities: it is a "melancholy"
place, decaying and smelly. "The whole thing is too queer—too

cold—too cruel." Nevertheless Yule, like Rosmer, is finally over-
come by its spirit of grim tradition; Covering End eventually becomes a symbol, like Rosmersholm, of the crushing values which
finally triumph. The ancient houses simply reclaim their own. Both
exert a compelling and irresistible pressure, an almost mystic compulsion, which causes Yule and Rosmer to lay aside their sincere
and eager Radicalism in the name of something more profound.

This analysis leads into a central point of the argument. The
triumph of traditional values in *Rosmersholm* and *Covering End*,
grimly vigorous as they are, is symbolised in the triumph of the
two old houses which are omnipresent in both works. In addition,
and this is the point that needs to be stressed, the use to which
James puts his symbol, and the way in which he exploits it,
closely follows the tissue of interrelations which connect image
and symbol in *Rosmersholm*. It is through an investigation of this
aspect of *Covering End* that we are led conveniently into a discussion of *The Spoils of Poynton*, as we shall see, for if we compare
symbolic function in the early and later versions of the story—
the one-act play and the nouvelle—it becomes apparent that between 1895 and 1898, while he was writing *The Spoils*, he acquired
a greater mastery of it than ever before. His advance is significant
enough to allow us to speak of a new kind of symbolism in his work.

Part of the explanation for this transformation lies in the net-
work of images and symbols, both little and great, which James
causes to accrete about the concept of the ancient mansion. Part
of Covering End, a living if decrepit limb, as it were, is the aged
retainer of the mansion, Chivers. In the play he is little more than
a piece of stage property, used to announce the entrance of major
characters, set the occasional scene and add, where necessary, a
little humour through his clumsy low-style dialect and aged fussi-
ness. In the nouvelle, however, he becomes identified, overtly and
implicitly, with all that is to be valued, and feared, in the crumbling mansion itself. He is "of the age of all the history that lurked
in all the corners" of the house. He imparts to everything he
touches its atmosphere and scale of implicit values, both aesthetic
and moral. His sigh "was like the creak of the wheel of time"—
an excellent example of the brilliant parenthetical touches by
which James, in the narrative form, was able to give to his characters and their surroundings that extension of symbolic meaning

and reference he was unable to put into a play. Thus he makes it possible for us to identify Chivers, a few moments later with the "sleeping echoes" which Mrs. Gracedew "fairly waked" when she calls out for him as she comes on stage for the first time. "Chivers gazed up at her in quick remembrance, half-dismayed, half-dazzled, of a duty neglected."

The long-neglected duty—a word fraught with special relevance and meaning in this nouvelle, as in *Rosmersholm*—is the veneration and preservation of the heritage, aesthetic and moral, that is Covering End's and England's ancient tradition. At so deep a level do all James's images link up that in this entrance we may detect an important point of the whole: Mrs Gracedew, an emissary from the New World (very like Lona Hessel in many respects) has come to revive and restore—and lay waste, as she warns Yule—England's antique treasures. In thus waking the echoes, the house and the old man simultaneously, Mrs Gracedew performs from the first the role she is to play throughout. Equally, when Chivers fumbles and drops the precious Chelsea pot—a moment of comedy in *Summersoft*, with his aged distress at the centre—the event takes on a symbolic significance comparable, in its power and relationship to the whole, with the smashing of the bowl in *The Golden Bowl*.

But if Chivers is linked symbolically to Covering End, so is Captain Yule. James begins with an inheritance but concludes with a complex of images and references which yield finally what we might term a compound symbol in which Yule, Chivers and Covering End stand as one. We are told, for example, that the Captain "was plainly as good in his own way as the old butler", and his sigh is described in words which are consciously designed to recall the striking image we noted earlier in connection with Chivers: "The sigh that dropped from [Captain Yule], however, was not quite void of tenderness. It might, for that matter, have been a long, sad creak, portending collapse, of some immemorial support of the Yules." Further, in the 'conversion' scene with Mrs Gracedew a deliberate ambiguity occurs which indicates, perhaps crudely, the close identification between Yule and his home which James was striving to effect. Mrs Gracedew creates a semantic confusion through the ambiguous use of the plural 'you' when referring to the house. Yule, understanding her word in the singular, assumes that she is in fact speaking of himself, and the whole incident permits a series of multi-level meanings to arise. Thus Yule, Covering End and Chivers are ultimately compounded into a single, interdependent yet flexible symbol of decaying, valuable, grim old England. This symbolic trinity, each part an independent entity yet each indissolubly part of the whole, may be compared with the composite tri-symbol of Rosmer, Beata and Rosmersholm which emerges in Ibsen's play. But again, what are important are not the correspondences of detail, though these are significant enough, but the close approximations of manner and technique. Certainly the self-conscious way in which James slots in crude and subtle interconnections between his 'idea' and the 'reality' of the action, recalls sharply not only his deep admiration for the close unity of form in *Little Eyolf*, *John Gabriel Borkman*, *Hedda Gabler* and other plays ("Ibsen's confined by completely constituted world, in which, in every case, the tissue of relations between the parts and the whole is of a closeness so fascinating"), but also his own acute analysis of the way it is achieved in *The Master Builder*. By the end of the nouvelle Yule, Chivers and Covering End are united as a symbol of the grand, decayed old Albion that is past but yet endures; for though they may have lost their way each continues to exist. When Mrs Gracedew, therefore, corrects Chivers's facts to the sightseers who stream across the stage in the last scene, his reply re-echoes in a chamber of symbolic implication: "I do seem, in them dark old centuries, to trip a little."

In his prefaces and notebooks James gives a very full account of the origins of *The Spoils of Poynton* and the development of its plot. At a Christmas party in 1893 Mrs Anstruther-Thompson mentioned to him the "small and ugly matter" of a young Scots laird who, after he married, evicted his mother from the home which she had spent her life beautifying. On taking possession, he found that she had removed many of the lovelier pieces and in the ensuing public squabble she maliciously declared that he was not the son of her late husband. James's creative imagination, fired by this anecdote, saw in it the possibility of a story in which to examine the "ugly English custom" of deposing the widowed mother. Clearly with the idea of an Ibsenesque social drama in mind (he saw the *donnée* as yielding "a little social and psychological picture") he sketched out a quick scenario in which the mother is motivated only by love for the *objets d'art* while the son is infatuated with a Philistine wife and totally uninterested in the sensitive girl of exquisite taste whom his mother wishes him to marry.

About eighteen months later, having promised Horace Scudder of the *Atlantic* three short stories, James revived the idea. The date was mid-May, 1895; a critical period, only three months after his discovery that the dramatist's key might fit the novelist's lock. Before turning back to his scenario he reminded himself in general that "more and more, everything of this kind I do must be a complete and perfect little drama. The little idea must resolve itself into a little action, and the little action into the *essential* drama aforesaid. *Voilà*. It is the way—it is perhaps the only way—to make some masterpieces. It is at any rate what I want to do." Two days later, when he resumed this entry, he had made some progress towards resolving the technical difficulty of turning his *donnée* into an action. He now envisaged the tale in "three chapters, like 3 little acts," each of which was to be fifty pages of manuscript in length. The whole story was not to be more than twenty thousand words.[1] Act I would deal with the son's want of taste, his mother's spiritual adoption of her own young girl (called at this stage Muriel Veetch) and would end with his disastrous marriage to the dreadful Nora Brigstock. Act II would describe Mrs Gereth's despair, her decision to cling to the treasures and her stealthy removal of the best to her dower-house. This act was to have as its climax the son's discovery of the theft. In Act III interest would shift to Muriel who, because she secretly loves the son, persuades his mother to return the spoils and so avoid the sordidness of a public quarrel. The dénouement of the whole piece was to be the "horrible, the atrocious conflagration" in which house and treasures are all finally destroyed.

By August, when James resumed his scenario, he had written some seventy pages of manuscript, nearly half the number he had originally allotted himself. At this stage, however, he had only reached the point where Owen and Mona come down to Poynton for the first time—the third of what were eventually twenty-two

[1] Mattheissen and Murdock, the joint editors of James's *Notebooks*, deduce this from the size of his handwriting.

chapters—and the marriage, originally planned to conclude the first act, has not yet taken place. James still believed nevertheless at this juncture that with concision he both should and would be able to stick to his initial plan. By mid-October, however, when he took up the story again, he realised that he would need at least another ten thousand words, and by the time he had finished the novel some eight months later, he had actually used another fifty thousand.

The notebooks provide the explanation for this sudden explosion. Between October, 1895 and April, 1896, as James worked on what had now become a novel, his interest shifted a third time, creating in the finished piece a second major emphasis. *The Spoils of Poynton* is a novel with a double centre, James's interest having moved from the conflict over the spoils to the conflict in Fleda's mind. The terms of her internal struggle are clearly delineated in his notes. Owen's marriage to Mona is to be conditional on his mother's returning the spoils, and it is to be within Fleda's power to prevent this happening. It was this conflict, James recorded, which helped constitute "whatever beauty I may put into the thing." Fleda, who deeply loves Owen, is heroically to resist the temptation to wreck his engagement. "The beauty of action and the poetry of effect," James wrote, "I can only, I think, find it just there." The novel eventually became the drama of Fleda's moral fineness—the picture, in a word, of a state of mind and soul, of chagrin and of despair.

The details of the finished work differed of course in many important respects from James's protean formulations over two or three years. Nevertheless, as his notes suggest, its final version, as in *The Other House*, is built up carefully scene by scene and falls clearly into three carefully constructed acts. Each has its own focus of locality and tone. The first is played out, with the exception of the first and last scenes, against the setting of Poynton itself. This achieves not only the unity of place and colour which James so admired in Ibsen, but serves also to establish the mansion as a powerful omnipresence and symbol after the analogy of *Covering End*. Further, as in *The Other House*, it acts as a prologue in which the *dramatis personae* are introduced and the central issues unfolded. Act II, which concludes with Fleda's being sent off to redeem Owen and Poynton, is staged entirely at Ricks, Mrs

Gereth's "melancholy" Essex dower-house. This act, comprising chapters VII to XII, but effectively scenes 7 to 10, initiates the confrontation of forces marshalled in Act I. The depressing influence of Ricks pervades this act, with its overtones of dispossession and faded life. It also contains the novel's emotional centre, Fleda's admission that she loves Owen, and concludes, as we have noted, on a pitch of high optimism and suspense as she sets off for London. Act III is the novel's longest, containing chapters XIII to XXII. The reasons for this extended treatment have already been given, but it should be pointed out that nevertheless the act itself is made up of only seven scenes (11 to 17) or, if we read the last two as being cast in the nature of an epilogue, of only five.

Each act, then, subdivides into a small number of tightly-organised scenes which carry the action. As I have indicated, they cut across normal chapter divisions which are used, in this case, as surrogates for the theatrical pause: emphases to stress a moment of high drama. An example would be the unexpected appearance of Mrs Brigstock at Fleda's London home just as Owen is about to declare himself at the end of the fourteenth chapter:

> The door opened, and the smutty maid, edging in, announced, "Mrs Brigstock!"

> XV

> Mrs Brigstock, in the doorway, stood looking from one of the occupants of the room to the other . . .

In addition, the abundance of stage techniques which James retained from his theatrical experience resulted in an important technical advance which enabled him, in this book and in subsequent novels, to create single scenes of some length. In *The Other House* he had attempted unsuccessfully to achieve this, and had thus been forced to rely heavily on improbable coincidence or authorial apology to explain the sudden reappearance or necessary departure of important figures. In *The Spoils of Poynton*, however, he prepared and executed his entrances and exits with far greater skill and with more imaginative use of the potentialities of narration. He disguises his manipulation by a simple convention. Instead of crudities such as Dennis Vidal's sudden discovery that he has left something in his trunk (thus leaving Rose *solus* so that she

78

can be discovered by Tony) he breaks up the pattern by slipping in, parenthetically, comments such as "the next day" or "the following week" before recording the apposite response. Thus by a simple time dislocation he is able to maintain the consistency of a single scene with question, answer and response presented in logical sequence.

A brief illustration of this process in action can be found in chapters IV and V. The climax to scene 3 is Mrs Gereth's polite, terrible rudeness as Owen and Mona leave Poynton after their visit. Fleda is shocked by her discourtesy, and turns on her with a scorching "How *could* you? Great God, how *could* you?" Mrs Gereth apologises, and again asks her what her feelings are towards Owen. The text continues, "On the second day, after the tide of emotion had somewhat ebbed, she said soothingly to her companion: 'But you would after all, marry him, you know, darling, wouldn't you, if that girl were not there? I mean of course if he were to ask you.' " Mrs Gereth's question and Fleda's response (refusal) are in reality part of the single scene which we picked up at the end of chapter III. There is a natural pause in the dialogue which is resumed when Mrs. Gereth breaks out, "with sudden rapture in the middle of the week: 'I know what they'll do: they *will* marry but they'll go and live at Waterbath!' " Owen's retort to this occurs "on the unforgettable day of his return" a few lines later; he makes it clear that this is simply wishful thinking on Mrs Gereth's part. Having made this point Owen exits—he returns to London. Fleda soliloquises mentally on this problem and then— one can almost hear James thinking "enter Mrs Gereth"—" 'I'll give up the house if they'll let me take what I require!'—that, on the morrow, was what Mrs Gereth's stifled night had qualified her to say with a tragic face at breakfast."

And so the scene continues. "The following week" Owen reappears to make his reply. What James is in effect doing—and elsewhere he does it without disguise—is carry on a running discussion between the three principals consistent and to the point in all respects, as one would expect on stage. Instead of having to create motivations and explanations for the necessary entrances and exits, however, he simply suggests that a few days have elapsed or that it is the following week. Mrs Gereth is painlessly removed; enter Owen.

Again, the notebooks bear out my point. While planning his novel James frequently noted down sequences of dialogue in play form and, as I've shown, he carried this into the story itself. All the important scenes in which great emotional intensity occur are written either in this form or on a straight-forward dramatic analogy, frequently with the minimum of authorial comment.

On the other hand I don't want to suggest that all the exchanges in *The Spoils of Poynton* are presented according to a facile theatre analogue such as we encounter in *The Awkward Age*. That novel is in many ways atypical of James's extended prompt-books, an experiment within an experiment, written after the manner of the *roman dialogue* and in the style of 'Gyp' and Henri Lavedan. In *The Spoils* he certainly invokes dialogue constructed in play form but, in addition, makes some use of indirect speech—what he called in his preface to *The Awkward Age* "dialogue in savourless dilution . . . boneless dispersion"—to render his scenes more acceptable than many of the highly-mannered and self-conscious episodes in *The Awkward Age*. I mean that he had learnt from the relative failure of *The Other House* to write for the eye and not for the ear.

The clash of generations is the theme of *The Spoils of Poynton*. Earlier I argued that the novel has a double centre, showing how as James worked he became progressively more concerned with the drama of Fleda's moral consciousness than with the struggle over Mrs Gereth's spoils. Despite this dual emphasis, however, he successfully united the disparate elements of his plot by relating both to the generational conflict. A series of embattled oppositions, each related to this theme and representing the collision of old and new, forms the basic structure of the whole. The story involves not only the struggle for material possession of the treasures of Poynton, but the conflict of antithetical life-styles. On one side stands Mrs Gereth, age, grace, tradition; on the other Mona Brigstock, youth, coarseness, modernity. Between the two, sharing qualities with each, stands Fleda Vetch, youth marshalled by age against youth.

Poynton and Waterbath are the two great opposing symbols in this encounter between modern vulgarity and traditional grace. Each represents, following the analogy of *Covering End*, not only a way of life but a generation and an attitude. The "dreadful . . .

horrible . . . intimate ugliness" of Waterbath, an ugliness "fundamental and systematic," is "the result of the abnormal nature of
the Brigstocks, from whose composition the principle of taste had
been extravagantly omitted. In the arrangement of their home some
other principle, remarkably active, but uncanny and obscure, had
operated instead, with consequences distressing to behold, consequences that took the form of a universal futility." In the same
way the loveliness of Poynton, qualified by the sterility which Fleda
finds there, expresses the abnormal nature of the Gereths. James
seems to be suggesting that an almost symbiotic relationship exists
between a family and its home, each influencing the other in
accordance with its nature until, by a process of mutual reinforcement, both become the same thing. Poynton and Waterbath are
hence, by definition, unique. James explained the process at the
climax of *Covering End*:

> Observe, above all, that you're in one of the most interesting
> old houses, of its type, in England; for which the ages have been
> tender and the generations wise; letting it change so slowly that
> there was always more left than taken—living their lives in it but
> letting it shape their lives!

As we have seen, the operation of this principle in narrative
action yielded the compound symbol—Yule, Chivers, the old house
—in close interrelation. By a similar process in *The Spoils of Poynton* James builds up his symbolic compounds with great skill. His
central concept, a very Ibsenic one, is that of the contagious taint.
Thus Mona, whose distorted aesthetic sense partly results in the
gaudy failure of Waterbath, is herself "exceptionally tainted" by
its vulgarity. Both are part of a single symbolic unit. Equally, however, at Poynton the "natural influence of a fine acquisition," as
Mrs Gereth expresses it, produces ultimately a contemptible mean-
ness of spirit and grasping avidity which is merely destructive. The
ambiguous fire at the end of the novel completes the point. Mrs
Gereth is, we are told, "despoiled of her humanity" by the place,
and brought to a numbed sterility by its crushing splendour:

> Poynton, moreover, had been an impossible place for producing;
> no active art could flourish there but a Buddhistic contemplation.
> It had stripped its mistress clean of all her feeble accomplishments;
> her hands were imbrued neither with ink nor with water-colour.

For all her rhetoric, Mrs Gereth is as deplorable in her own way as Mona. A sort of black contagious magic allies objects of great ugliness or beauty in the novel; and though it is quite clear which James prefers, if called upon to choose, he is careful to show that the process is a vicious one in both cases. Thus Mrs Gereth herself despoils Poynton; but is herself despoiled by it. By the same token, she overreacts to the threat of Mona who, as Fleda remarks, "wouldn't after all smash things nor burn them up." What Mrs Gereth objects to is that "Mona would approach Poynton in the spirit of a Brigstock and in the spirit of a Brigstock she would deal with her acquisition."

Mrs Gereth's assumption that Mona is a predator and destroyer is a major provocation of the crisis. She speaks of "poor Mona's taint" as if to mention it "were almost a violation of decency." Fleda later goes on to shrewdly observe that "perhaps almost any girl would hate a person who should be so markedly averse to having anything to do with her." Mrs Gereth fears the Brigstocks because she realises, with the shock of self-recognition, that their ambition and avidity match her own; that the threat they offer is of the same ruthless kind she presented the established collections of her youth. Poynton is hardly an ancestral seat; it is the creation of a single generation. Mrs Gereth, ruthless, determined, with luck and talent on her side, is the builder of a beautiful home who, in vigorous middle age, is forced by the inevitable processes of time into a posture of defence—of defiance—against just such an attack as she herself has consistently made. As Fleda reflects, it was fascinating "to hear this genuine English lady, fresh and fair, young in the fifties, declare with gaiety and conviction that she was herself the greatest Jew who ever tracked a victim." For Mrs Gereth, therefore, Mona's great crime is her modernity, her youth. She represents the rising generation; this is the basis of her threat. The generations tread very closely on one another's heels in *The Spoils of Poynton*.

The key to the book is of course the relationship between Owen and Fleda, who represent the possibility of a new synthesis in which youth and spiritual integrity will be allied. Just as Owen is both of, and not of, Poynton Park, so Fleda, although "a spirit of the same family" as Mrs Gereth, is uncorrupted by the passion for ownership. Her spirit is larger, undemeaned: "Almost as much as Mrs Gereth's her taste was her life, but her life was somehow the larger for it." That this new synthesis is finally unrealised, and the treasures destroyed, is as much the fault of Mrs Gereth's crude insensitivity as Mona's pushing ambition. Each operates, in its own obscure manner, to erode the possibilities of love: these are the final spoils of Poynton.

The argument I have been trying to sustain so far rests, with regard to James's submission to Ibsen, on the demonstration of indirect influence. *The Spoils of Poynton*, as we have seen, was written quite consciously according to a play analogy and it includes in addition many techniques and innovations which can be shown to have derived from Jamesian imitations of Ibsenic tragedy. The point can be taken further, however, for as with the bulk of James's post-theatre narrative prose, Ibsen's exemplative presence in the novel can be detected in detail as well as in broad outline. In particular terms, the theme of *The Spoils of Poynton*, and the predicament which Mrs. Gereth finds herself confronting, have much in common with the theme of *The Master Builder* and the situation of Solness. As we saw earlier, James's intense interest in this play was contemporaneous with his original formulations of the novel and, as I shall argue, appears to have affected the initial emphases of the plot.

The clash of generations is the theme of *The Master Builder*. The series of oppositions which go to make up the structure of the play represents the conflict between old and new, between youth and middle age, in a way which strikingly recalls *The Spoils of Poynton*. Solness's hostility to Ragnar, like Mrs Gereth's to Mona, is both excessive and the provocation of the final crisis. He is being forced to "make room", to get out; and as he confesses to Hilda, "I've begun to be so terribly afraid—so terribly afraid of the younger generation . . . I tell you the younger generation will one day come and thunder at my door!"

James himself saw the play in these terms. So far as he was concerned, Solness was a "prosperous architect of Christiania who, on reaching a robust maturity, encounters his fate all in the opening of a door." As Hilda crosses Solness's threshold, says James, she "lets in a great deal more than herself"; she becomes the "indirect form" of his fate. He is "all memories and hauntings and bondages", a figure doomed from the rise of the curtain; but she is "all health and curiosity and youthful insolence," willing to help her beloved master builder in his struggle against the rising young, yet unwittingly the cause of his destruction.

The contrasts of the play are clearly drawn. On one side stands Solness, age, a beautiful but sterile achievement; on the other Ragnar Brovik, youth, modernity, the new generation with an architectural blueprint for the future. Between these two sets of embattled positions stands Hilda Wangel, sharing simultaneously Solness's values and Ragnar's youth. Under her guidance the master builder yields first to one demand, then another, until he finally destroys himself. Yet right to the end, like Mrs Gereth, Solness believes that he may have successfully marshalled youth against youth.

The parallels with *The Spoils of Poynton* are of course not exact. Solness's career contains an element of self-compromise absent from Mrs Gereth's, while Mona presents a more absolute threat to an objective canon of taste than Ragnar. The aesthetic terms in which both Mrs Gereth and Solness condemn the new genera-tion, however, are certainly similar: each claims that youth has come only to destroy, that it will render merely ugliness. My point nevertheless is not that Mrs Gereth is Solness anglicised, but that as James worked on his novel the insistent example of *The Master Builder* gradually transformed the emphases of his characterisa-tion and story. The Mrs Gereth we encounter in the finished fiction has little in common with the hysterical widow who, in Mrs Anstruther-Thompson's anecdote, denounced her son in a fit of spite as no child of her late husband's. She is instead a strong central figure, defiant in middle age, who shares a number of important defining qualities with Solness.

In an early response to the play James conceived of Solness as a woman. He was writing to Mrs Hugh Bell about Elizabeth Robins's disappointment that its leading part was given to a man; she had hoped so intensely that *The Master Builder* might be another *Hedda Gabler*. James wrote:

> Hilda will evidently come out, greatly, in the next acts, but she will come out further from Miss E. And the fact remains that the quinquagenarian architect *must* be the heroine—Miss Elizabeth must do *him*.

In *The Spoils of Poynton* Mrs Gereth is the quinquagenarian architect who *has*, in a sense, become the heroine; quite like Solness she is ruthless in acquisition and triumph, but diminished in victory. As James puts it, "The truth was simply that all Mrs Gereth's scruples were on one side and that her ruling passion had in a manner despoiled her of her humanity." Solness has been despoiled in the same way. His ambition renders him incapable of viewing Old Brovik, Ragnar, Kaia, even his own wife, as anything other than as the means to an end. His defiance of the inevitable, like Mrs Gereth's, is characteristic. Youth, in the form of Hilda on the one hand and Fleda on the other, is to be turned against itself. The final irony is the same as the two young women, eager to assist, unknowingly encompass the final catastrophe. Both Hilda and Fleda persuade their master builders to bow before the inexorable—Solness gives Ragnar his chance and Mrs Gereth returns the spoils. The final moments in either drama, as both girls watch helplessly, are the symbolic and literal consequence.

What I have been trying to do in this chapter is to indicate, as its title suggests, some of the immediate formulations which James's initial reactions to Ibsen gave rise to. Rather than concentrate on a single story or novel, I have attempted to trace a variety of approaches to the problem of his narrative use of Ibsen: *The Other House* shows him in his most dramatising and plagiaristic mood; *Covering End* displays his critical intelligence and technical responsiveness at its fullest stretch; and *The Spoils of Poynton*, the best of his works from this period, illustrates how both served to liberate his talents from the technical and creative cul-de-sac into which he had been led by 1895.

This brings the first part of my argument to a convenient close. In the second section of this book I will try to show how James continued to draw on his earlier experiences to create the finest narrative prose fictions of his later career. Almost everything that he was subsequently to achieve was indebted, as we will see, to his theatre and post-theatre experiments; for as he himself observed only six years before his death while working on *The Ivory Tower*:

. . . I see in other words my Exposition made perfect—see the thing as almost the Prologue, after the manner in which the first

Book is the Prologue in *The Other House*. Oh, blest *Other House*, which gives me thus at every step a precedent, a support, a divine little light to walk by.

This is an astonishing statement for a writer to make of a neglected and self-contemned novel. Clearly it indicates his awareness, not only of the impetus afforded by the dramatic method, but of the creative departure ("at every step") in terms of subject matter and approach which it marked. The light cast by our discussion of this novel will I hope illuminate the rest of his career.

PART TWO

The Spoils of Ibsen

3

Ibsen Turns the Screws

In a remarkable essay called "Henry James as Freudian Pioneer", Oscar Cargill argues that James's Preface to *The Turn of the Screw* contains a hint that there were sources for the tale other than Archbishop Benson's now-famous anecdote. Cargill's reference is to the passage where James, having recounted the story of his dinner with the Archbishop, and the telling of the anecdote of the dead servants, goes on to comment, "Such was the private source of *The Turn of the Screw*; and I wondered, I confess, why so fine a germ, gleaming there in the wayside dust of life, had never been deftly picked up." Cargill, however, reminds us that both A. C. Benson and his brother always emphatically denied that the little story was ever part of their father's repertoire; and he goes on to suggest that there were perhaps public sources, that is, things in print, matter generally available, which played their part as well. These observations are intriguing, especially when we take them in conjunction with James's remark in a letter to F. W. H. Myers that he had been fully reconciled, when writing the tale, to make use of any means at hand, even the imitation of someone else's work, to render his artistic point effective. I shall of course argue that among these public sources were the plays of Ibsen—in particular, I shall suggest that *Ghosts*, Ibsen's powerful and shocking tragedy of corrupt innocence, exerted a particularly important shaping pressure on the direction James's story eventually took. It is not my argument that James took *Ghosts* as his starting point, but that, as he worked, so the dramatic mould in which he quite consciously cast the nouvelle, and his awareness of Ibsen's drama and his admiration for that achievement, profoundly affected his conception.

In both *Ghosts* and *The Turn of the Screw* evil seeks to lay hold of the present. It is dramatised in ghostly presences which, as the action proceeds, reveal themselves as having taken possession of innocent children, working from within to encompass their destruction. Adults are apparently immune from the raptorial apparitions; their role is that of fruitless protection.

Archbishop Benson's anecdote, as James records it in his notebooks, postulates both the children and the ghosts, but the importance and weight of the central thematic concern is omitted altogether. James began with a conventional ghost story but finished with a moral statement whose terms are symbolised in the apparitions and the children. The point of the original anecdote was that the wicked servants return as spirits, not to continue the process of contagion, but to lure the children (age and number unspecified) to their deaths. James noted:

> The servants *die* (the story vague about the way of it) and their apparitions, figures, return to haunt the house *and* the children, to whom they seem to beckon, whom they invite and solicit, from across dangerous places, the deep ditch of a sunk fence, etc.—so that the children may destroy themselves, lose themselves, by responding, by getting into their power. So long as the children are kept from them, they are not lost; but they try and try and try, these evil presences, to get hold of them. It is a question of the children "coming over to where they are."

This is surely distinct from the finished work whose point is that Peter Quint destroys Miles from within; he is already in possession. In the last days the governess gives Miles his liberty, surrenders him not to death but, as it were, to corruption. Miles finally dies of pollution from within, his moral rottenness a fever which burns him up.

The Turn of the Screw thus deals with the corruption of innocence. At the centre of the tale is the apparent purity of the children already tainted by the appalling depravity of Peter Quint and Miss Jessel. "Their more than earthly beauty, their absolutely unnatural goodness," says the governess of the children, "it's a game; it's a policy and a fraud!" And when Mrs Grose asks why the two ghosts should seek to corrupt the children the governess replies, "For the love of that evil that, in those dreadful days, the pair put into them. And to ply them with that evil still, to keep up the work of demons, is what brings the others back."

These ghosts are not the conventional figures of Gothic melo-drama. They are symbols of an encroaching evil and have little resemblance, as James himself remarked in his Preface, to the ghosts of popular imagination. Peter Quint and Miss Jessel, in life and death, are emblematic of certain immoral qualities and it is these, more than their 'ghostliness' which are important for James and his tale. Although their apparitions do frighten us, as I'm sure he intended, it is not their spookiness which does so but their power for infinite moral corruption. James noted that they were meant to make the situation "reek with the air of Evil", a capital-ised abstraction, and in the tale itself Peter Quint is repeatedly a deathly figure, a "horror", and Miss Jessel a "horror of horrors", black as midnight. Their unseen presences create in both the governess and Mrs Grose an unreasoning terror, their impending manifestation a sense of confrontation with some dreadful, name-less power, "something which gathers and crouches . . . the spring of a beast." When she learns of Quint's long, corrupting associa-tion with Miles, the governess feels "a sudden quickness of dis-gust", and demands of Mrs Grose: "You weren't afraid of any-thing else? Not of his effect . . . on innocent precious little lives?"

It becomes clear that the apparitions in the finished tale have more in common with Ibsen's ghosts than with Archbishop Ben-son's weird spectres. Captain Alving and Mrs Engstrand, having created by their indulgent sensuality an ethos thick with corrup-tion, return after their deaths as the embodiment of evil. Miles, the little boy who dies in James's drama, does not of course suffer from congenital syphilis like Oswald Alving; but rather, through-out the latter half of the action, and increasingly as the climax approaches, he displays symptoms of physical decline which suggest that his moral condition, of which the illness is an emblem, is very close to Oswald's. He is repeatedly imaged as a sick child, "some wistful patient in a children's hospital", given to sudden fevers and languid movements of the head. His "sick little headshake", and recurring droopings and saggings at the end, recall vividly Oswald's decline during the final act of *Ghosts*. Further, his "sud-den fever", the "tremendous pulse of his little heart", and the "per-fect dew of sweat on his lovely childish forehead", appear to look back in some measure to Oswald's striking description of the pipe-smoking episode in *Ghosts* which images the process of contagious corruption at Rosenvold. Trapped on his father's knee Oswald was compelled to smoke away at his pipe until he "turned quite pale . . . the perspiration stood in great drops on my forehead . . . then I was sick . . ."

This incident prefigures, as Oswald's entrance with his father's pipe suggests, his moral destruction by an analogous process some twenty years later. In both cases his father's moral poison, innocently inhaled, corrupts and sickens him. In both cases the process is imaged dramatically in symptoms of physical disease. This is a powerful histrionic technique, and one which Ibsen was frequently to use. In his plays bodily disorders characteristically reflect moral conditions—Solness's dizziness, for example, or Dr Rank's spinal tuberculosis. Engstrand's bad leg would be another instance. To encounter in a late Henry James nouvelle a similar process and comparable image in the thematic context already discussed, however, suggests to my mind a conscious relationship. Miles's illness and death, and Flora's abrupt fever, are both images of moral corrosion which we may, I think reasonably, trace back to Ibsen.

I have so far argued that the spectres in both pieces represent similar qualities of depravity and evil, and that their power is displayed in the moral and physical havoc they are able to wreak in the children. A corollary point, however, and it is central to both works, is the assumption (treated as an axiom—but disregarded in *What Maisie Knew*) that an environment dense with sexual corruption will contaminate children to the point of death. It is thus irrelevant to the 'meaning' of *Ghosts* that Regina, although Oswald's younger sister, has not inherited their father's syphilis. Her corruption, as a consequence of the same spiritual contagion, is moral; like Flora, she cleaves to the female spectre. She finally exits, probably to become a prostitute in Engstrand's brothel, with the bitter remark, "Oh! What must be must be. If Oswald takes after his father I take after my mother, I daresay." It is a turn of the screw. Brother and sister have been both, in their own ways, morally and physically destroyed by the corrupting presence of the Past.

In James's tale the pattern is repeated. The story deals, as we have seen, with the corrosion of innocence by an obscene and depraved environment. The corruption at Bly is a miasma which is "in the place itself", Quint's ghost is a "living, detestable, dangerous presence" which "poisons" the atmosphere and drives the two children "mad." The relationship between himself and Miss Jessel was the most horrid possible; both were "infamous . . . depraved", communicating their moral taintedness by mere association. Flora, a pretty child of eight, becomes an "old, old, woman . . . common and almost ugly." Bly itself eventually becomes a "prison", from which Flora, like Regina, just escapes; Miles is trapped inside as Quint stands white-faced at the window, his captor, judge and executioner.

So manifold are the echoes between this theme and its resolution, and the corresponding elements in *Ghosts*, that one is compelled, when examining them within the context of what we know of James's interests and ambitions at the time, to postulate the probability of influence. In so doing we would not be overlooking that *The Other House, Owen Wingrave, The Pupil, What Maisie Knew* and *The Awkward Age* all deal with this same theme in some measure. *What Maisie Knew*, in particular, demonstrates the contrary conclusion when the child emerges more or less morally unscathed from the depraved environment in which she finds herself; and in *The Awkward Age* she is shown to be superior to it, Maisie grown up. During these years, as I suggested earlier, James moved away from the simpler and more traditional antitheses of America and Europe, which characterised his treatment of the theme in the novels of the pre-theatre phase, to a more profound consideration of the problem of evil. In the novels and tales of the middle phase he found in European society itself adequately antagonistic elements, and blacker tones than ever before, with which to express his sense of moral conflict. Further, it was Ibsen who at this time provided him with the terms of his discussion, as I hope I have shown; the form taken by a nouvelle such as *The Turn of the Screw* echoes Ibsen because in a play like *Ghosts* he showed James how to express his sense of evil in contemporary society without having to resort to Hawthornesque allegory. We will come back to this point in the next chapter.

I should perhaps, before proceeding, record my reasons, despite Edmund Wilson's ingenious account of the tale in "The Ambiguity of Henry James", for accepting the literal existence of the ghosts.

One does so, of course, with regret; the glory, as I think Oscar Cargill once observed, is all on the other side. But unfortunately, apart from the internal inconsistencies in Mr Wilson's own argument, the publication more than twenty years ago of James's notebooks cut away most of the ground from beneath his feet. James's notes made it clear that his *donnée* concerned real apparitions and, although to my mind this does not preclude subsequent modification, it does support James's other comments in letters and prefaces. In addition to this—a more important point—the Prologue to the tale itself provides us with sufficient evidence to call the whole Freudian reading into question. Douglas, the possessor of the manuscript which contains the history, goes to considerable lengths to establish unambiguously the governess's sanity, emotional stability, and kindliness; she was, we are told, his sister's governess in the years following the incident at Bly, a "charming . . . agreeable . . . awfully clever and nice" mature lady.

To question or ignore this statement, as Mr Wilson does, or to overlook the obvious implication that the governess received the best of references from Miles's guardian, seems simply gratuitous to me. James clearly intended by it that we should both trust the governess and the facts of her tale—he had seen Mr Wilson coming. As a dramatic action the story is, I believe, to be taken literally.

The first notebook entries for *The Turn of the Screw* go back to January, 1895, exactly one week after the collapse of *Guy Domville*. This is an interesting point, for like most of James's tales and novels conceived during this period but executed later, its scenic construction and arrangement bear out the expection that it was the dramatic form which was primarily in his mind when he wrote it. The plot is arranged in five approximately equal 'acts' and a prologue. This prologue is extremely important, not only because, as we have seen, it establishes the credentials of the governess, but also because it establishes the crucial relation between audience and actor. As I have already suggested, James's failure in the theatre was partly responsible for his development of the theory of the central reflecting consciousness. His retort to Victorian audiences who would not or could not respond to the nuances which he, James, detected in a glance or unfinished sentence, was to compel them to view the action through his own eyes. In effect, he made

his audience Henry James. Characteristic of his later manner is
the controlling intellect or observer, James's ideal spectator, who
reports to the reader and corrects his responses and judgments.
This is one of the functions of the anonymous governess. The
fact that her story is read to a fireside audience is an essential
dimension. The reader is placed within the group around the fire;
he is part of the audience viewing the action through her interposing vision. This relates to the fact that the tale is subsequently
executed within that strong theatrical mould which, as we have
seen and shall see, shaped for better or ill James's later work.
The following brief analysis describes this process in *The Turn of
the Screw*.

Act I, which follows the short, audience-setting prologue, is
made up, essentially, of four scenes. All the acts, with the exception of the second, comprise four scenes. Act II, which is very
tightly structured, has three. The first scene of the play, following
the governess's entrance, is an extended dialogue through scenic
disguise, after the fashion James had perfected in *The Spoils of
Poynton*, between herself and Mrs Grose. They discuss the two
children, and especially Miles. The second scene describes the first
appearance of Peter Quint, and the third his second visitation at
the window. The fourth is the exchange between Mrs Grose and
the narrator which concludes with the dramatic revelation that
Quint is dead; and that he has therefore risen again from the
grave. This brings the act powerfully to a close. It also recalls, in
tone and manner, the chilling conclusion to the first act of *Ghosts*
when Mrs Alving, "wild-eyed and starting with terror", tells
Manders: "Ghosts! . . . The couple from the conservatory—risen
again!"

The parallels are not simply those of melodrama. Both scenes
dramatise the persistence of moral corruption in an apparently
purified world; the evil has contrived to re-emerge, in a ghostly
presence, and thus continue its process of contagious immundicity.
In both cases sexual depravity comes once again to interpose itself
between the living and their children: a dramatised moral evil
which is inexorable in its power. I am reluctant at this stage to
attempt to take these parallels too far, but they are suggestive and
may take on a greater significance when we have examined the
two pieces in more detail.

Act II, as I have said, is even more tightly structured than Act I. Of its three scenes the first picks up the action and dialogue where Act I concludes, developing its implications in much the same way as the first scene in Act II of *Ghosts*; the second contains the 'sea of Azof' episode in which Miss Jessel's ghost appears for the first time; and the third is an extended dialogue between the governess and Mrs Grose which closes on a note of deep apprehension and despair.

The third act includes sections IX to XIII. Scene 1 describes the appearance of Quint on the stairways and contains the governess's discovery that little Flora is out of bed watching Miles. Scene 2 is an exchange with Miles about this incident and Scene 3 another discursive and analytic dialogue with Mrs Grose. This interview leads easily and naturally into the concluding soliloquy which makes up section XIII. Its effect is to draw together the existing tensions and create, in preparation for the violence of the conclusion, the necessary suspense and fear.

Act IV, although of the same length as Act II, is made up of the usual four scenes. This act, despite its comparative brevity, is packed with action, impelling the drama towards its climax. The first scene, which heralds the beginning of the final crisis, as the governess notes, is the exchange between herself and Miles as they walk to church one Sunday morning. The second is her discovery, when she returns alone and unexpectedly, of Miss Jessel in the schoolroom; and the third is a discussion with Mrs Grose about this incident. Scene 4 is the terrifying interview with Miles which concludes with his scream and the doused candle. Its shock is roughly comparable with the orphanage fire in *Ghosts*; the destructive power of the living dead manifests itself directly, a signal that the climax is at hand.

The final act contains that climax. Once again, we have four scenes. The first is brief and introductory: the governess and Mrs Grose are beguiled by Miles's piano playing and then discover to their horror that Flora has disappeared. Scene 2 is their pursuit and recovery of the little girl, and contains the depths of the governess's despair. The third scene describes her decision, taken in conjunction with Mrs Grose, to get Flora away from the poison at Bly, and the fourth, which contains the drama's climax, portrays the final struggle between the governess and Quint for the soul of little Miles. This scene, and the play itself, concludes with Miles's death. As the dawn breaks she finds him dead in her arms:

> They are in my ears still, his supreme surrender of the name and his tribute to my devotion. "What does it matter now, my own?— what will he *ever* matter? I have you," I launched at the beast, "but he has lost you forever!" Then, for the demonstration of my work, "There, *there*!" I said to Miles.
>
> But he had already jerked straight round, stared, glared again, and seen but the quiet day. With the stroke of the loss I was so proud of, he uttered the cry of a creature hurled over an abyss, and the grasp with which I recovered him might have been that of catching him in his fall. I caught him, yes. I held him—it may be imagined with what a passion; but at the end of a minute I began to feel what it truly was that I held. We were alone with the quiet day, and his little heart, dispossessed, had stopped.

This passage might almost be read as Mrs Alving's account of the conclusion of *Ghosts*. The governess's possessive protective words at the beginning of the passage echo in tone Mrs Alving's, spoken as she bends over Oswald:

> It has been a dreadful fancy of yours, Oswald—nothing but a fancy. All this excitement has been too much for you. But now you shall have a long rest; at home with your mother, my own blessed boy. Everything you point to you shall have, just as when you were a child. There now. That crisis is over now. You see how easily it passed. Oh! I was sure it would—and do you see, Oswald, what a lovely day we're going to have? Brilliant sunshine! Now you'll really be able to see your home.

Mrs Alving's reassuring words are a prelude to the final tragedy, a brief moment of peace and tranquillity before the *gengangere* launch their last, fatal attack. As she looks down at Oswald she finds victory snatched from her in the very instant of hope.

The parallels between this scene and the last moments of *The Turn of the Screw* need not be too heavily emphasised at this stage. Both represent the climax of a struggle against moral evil: defeat in the hour of apparent victory. The moral rot, dramatised in the ghosts and the physical illness of both children, finally claims its victim. Furthermore, the atmosphere and settings of both scenes are strikingly alike. As dawn breaks through the windows of the lonely country houses, the two mortally stricken children, folded in mothering arms, are finally destroyed. The horror draws part of its strength from the structured antitheses in both pieces: apparent beauty and inner corruption, the clean sun and the rotten home. Finally, the tenderness of the women and the violence of the conclusion, the handsome faces of the children and the rot within.

In his *Ibsen's Dramatic Method*, John Northam has a useful and accurate analysis of the visual symbolism in *Ghosts*. His main point is that the encircling gloom at Rosenvold, which symbolises the evil qualities of moral corruption, sanctimony and outmoded convention, is vitiated only by a still, small candle gleam, associated with light and youth, which, as the action progresses, eventually goes out. He puts it this way:

> To summarize: gloom of the set has come to mean obscurity of convention, hypocrisy and depravity, all of which attach themselves to the late Captain and his memorial, the Orphanage. Engstrand has come to symbolize the vicious aspects of the exterior; Manders is the blinkered conventionalist; Mrs Alving claims to think freely, but she makes no protest against the grim background; Regina and the flowers in the conservatory combine to suggest the only youthful note of beauty.

Later he notes the symbolic significance of Regina's appearance with the lamp and the irony as, at dawn, Mrs Alving extinguishes it.

The process of moral corruption suggested by these visual images seems clear enough. The pervasive evil which corrupts Oswald and Regina appears, at the play's outset, to be confined to the wicked world outside; the home is a haven. The driving "devil's rain" associated with Engstrand apparently stops at the windows; Manders remarks, as he enters, "Ah! It's a comfort to get safe under cover." As the act proceeds, however, it is revealed that the corruption is already within. Captain Alving, as his widow reveals to the deeply-shocked Pastor, had brought it all into the home itself. This was his greatest moral crime: to have brought the mephitic gloom inside. Oswald was sent away because "it seemed to me the child must be poisoned by merely breathing the air of this polluted home." Rosenvold has been invaded; like Oswald, who has only apparently kept both his inner and outer selves unharmed, the home is *vermoulu*, worm-eaten, and rotten to the core. This point is dramatised during the crucial closing moments when Mrs Alving, exalting over Rosenvold's elutriation through her husband's death, discovers to her horror that his ghost has risen, returned to haunt, corrupt and finally destroy. The invasion is complete.

From this point onwards in the play the darkness becomes intense. Act II opens with the stage direction, "the mist still lies heavy over the landscape", and the ghosts are increasingly associated with it. They are now both within and without, "as thick as the sand of the sea", and omnipotent because "we are, one and all, so pitifully afraid of the light" which could banish them forever. There is not "a single ray of sunlight the whole day", and Oswald complains: "It's so dark here! And this ceaseless rain! It may go on week after week for months together. Never to get a glimpse of the sun! I can't recollect ever having seen the sun shine all the times I've been at home." Mrs Alving's response to this is to have Regina bring in the faint table lamp which burns on the set from this point onwards until the play's closing moments.

The third act opens with the direction: "The room as before. The lamp is still burning on the table. It is dark out of doors; there is only a faint glow from the conflagration in the background to the left." These details are symbolically significant. The doors are open, a sign that resistance to the invaders has ended. The lamp still burns, faintly, but the outer darkness is as impenetrable as ever: the orphanage fire glows only dimly, unable to relieve the gloom and is, indeed, in many ways a part of it. As the act proceeds Mrs Alving comes to understand her own culpability in the corruption at Rosenvold. Her husband, filled as a young man with that recurring Ibsenic "joy of life", was himself slowly destroyed by the outer darkness and she, his wife, might have saved him. She expresses her realisation in terms of the play's central image: "Your poor father found no outlet for the overpowering joy of life that was in him. And I brought no brightness into his home." Then, as the play draws to its close, she symbolically turns down the glowing table lamp as Oswald, crying for the sun, surrenders to the night.

Ibsen used the same antithetical symbols five years later in *Rosmersholm*, a drama which Henry James, as we have already seen, studied in great detail and drew on in depth. This play is also, like *Ghosts*, a "duel between light and darkness", as Northam expresses it, represented in similar terms of faintly-glowing, extinguishable table-lamps symbolising enlightenment and freedom. As the action proceeds the evil triumphs, snuffing out the lights and drawing the protagonists to their deaths in the gloom. The ghosts, although they do not appear on stage except in symbolic form—Rebecca's white shawl, for instance—are of a more traditional variety, manifesting themselves in one guise as a horrid white horse. In *The Lady from the Sea*, which we will look at more closely presently, the ghostly Stranger actually appears before the audience.

The Turn of the Screw makes use of a similar set of light/dark contrasting images. More significantly, perhaps, it uses them in the same way as in *Ghosts* and *Rosmersholm*, and makes through them the same moral point. The nouvelle's opening suggests the surge-and-ebb pattern which is to be repeated throughout: "I remember the whole beginning as a succession of flights and drops, a little see-saw of the right throbs and the wrong." The first day glows with a magnificent sunny lightness: filled with "bright flowers" and a "golden sky." It is only in the "fading dusk" that the governess hears sounds "less natural and not without but within" that make her uneasy. She comments. ". . . it is only in the light, or the gloom I should rather say, of other and subsequent matters that they now come back to me."

The children themselves are at first "radiant", gazing up at her with "a great childish light" and a "great glow of freshness" which, like the golden day, belies the dark corruption unnaturally within. This series of images, and the images of darkness which succeed it, establishes the crucial relation between light and moral beauty on the one hand, and darkness and spiritual depravity on the other.

It may be objected at this point, however, that after all light and darkness are fairly conventional moral images; and that, further, Henry James, unlike ourselves, never had the advantage of reading Dr Northam's excellent little book. But James perfectly well understood the visual and symbolic correlations of Ibsen's dramatic method, and in his perceptive essays he made it clear that his grasp was profound. In 1897, for example, he observed that in Ibsen's drama "the spirit is a lamp within us, glowing through what the world and the flesh make of us as through a ground-glass shade." And of *Little Eyolf* and *John Gabriel Borkman* he went on in the same essay to remark that each was a *"chassez-croisez"* of burning spiritual lamps, glowing "as in tasteless parlours, with the flame practically exposed. There are no shades in the house, or the Norwegian ground-glass is singularly clear."

In *Ghosts* and *Rosmersholm* the ground-glass of what the world and the flesh make of us progressively darkens until the spiritual flame is put out. The metaphor is repeated in *The Turn of the Screw*. When Quint first appears it is as the sun is setting "at the end of a long June day" which his presence seems to strike with death. An intense hush falls, and the rooks "stopped cawing in the golden sky." By the time the governess re-enters the house "darkness had quite closed in." Her sense of alarm, however, is like a "dawn", and the house itself is, for the moment, "bright in the lamplight." From this point onwards, however, the impenetrable darkness outside looms with increasing ominousness. Quint's second appearance, in Scene 3, takes place on an evening further darkened by rain and a chilling wind. This is the authentic rain of *Ghosts*; it is interminable and drives with unnatural force. The sky remains grey after the rain stops although, we are told, "the afternoon light still lingered". It is a moment of balance, for the threatening gloom is temporarily illuminated by the governess's "flash" of understanding that Quint is looking for Miles. It is notable that towards the end of the book she recalls this momentary gleam, but dismisses it as a "flash of something it would scarce have done to call light." Later, in Scene 4 of the first act, she recounts to Mrs Grose her experience with Quint in terms of what has by now become the nouvelle's central image. Mrs Grose asks her to say when she first saw the ghostly apparition, and she replies:

> "About the middle of the month. At this same hour."
> "Almost as dark," said Mrs Grose.
> "Oh, no, not nearly. I saw him as I see you."

The darkness and evil are progressive. As Quint comes nearer his shadow looms larger; the children's innocence is now seen to be "clouded." At this point James begins, in the familiar Ibsen manner which we began to trace in the first chapter, to integrate his imagery with the banal furnishing of the provincial country home. By this process he extends it until it takes on the force of symbol, investing the entire tale with a tremendous sense of conflict and moral rending. This is what F. O. Mattheissen described as James's ability to "bind together his imaginative effects by subtly recurrent images of a thematic kind", and to "extend metaphor into a symbol." My point would be that James borrowed this process from Ibsen, whose own symbolic manner, I have already shown, follows this procedure exactly. Furthermore, in *The Turn of the Screw*, as in the other novels and tales I have discussed in detail, James appears to have borrowed not only Ibsen's technique but its exact terms as well. The horror of the story's central events draws its power from the associations which, as in *Ghosts* and *Rosmersholm*, are allowed to accrete about the antithetical concepts of light and shadow. These associations—moral corruption, the Past and sexual disgrace in conflict with youth, freedom and beauty—invest the daily objects at Bly, Rosenvold and Rosmersholm with unique symbolic strength.

Quint's third manifestation occurs at the dead of night when the governess, filled with foreboding, sits reading by the light of two candles. This scene and its setting have the same symbolic significance as the stage directions from *Ghosts* already discussed—an encroaching darkness broken only by feeble human means. Sensing that something is astir in the house the governess takes up one of her candles and steps out into the gloom "on which my light made little impression." At the head of the stair three things happen almost at once: she sees Quint, inside the house for the first time; her light "under a bold flourish" goes out; and she realises that dawn is about to break. The significance and power of this episode are felt simultaneously on a literal and symbolic level, each intersecting with the other to create a situation of enormous tension. The snuffed candle and its former feeble light register the force and strength of Quint's darkness into which, the next minute, he vanishes. Nevertheless it is a blackness not wholly impenetrable—the battle is not yet lost. The morning twilight is cold but faint, "with a glimmer in the high glass and another in the polish of the oak stair." At this moment of supreme danger, when Quint and his evil have invaded the very house itself, the governess discovers that, at least at this point, "dread had unmistakably quitted me and that there was nothing in me that didn't meet and measure him." She returns to her room to find the second candle still burning. By its light she discovers that Flora has left her bed and is looking out into the early dawn. Mistakenly the governess believes that she will be able to make Flora confess, make her bring the secret literally, figuratively and symbolically out into the light. She fails; and on the next occasion she wakes to find that the light she had left burning has been put out. Worse, it is Flora herself who has extinguished it. The governess's pathetic response to this new darkness is to strike a match; a tiny spark of hope and light, all that remains of the great golden sky and sunshine of the opening scenes. The darkness within, she now notes, is deeper than that outside. When she brings Miles back inside she has to lead him through deep shadows and "dark spaces" to his room where the moonlight serves only to make the gloom more melancholy. Even light itself comes to take on a sinister quality. The children's radiant glow, as the tale progresses, subtly modulates to a harsh glitter which dazzles the governess by its brittle shininess and prevents her from seeing the depths of their inner despair. The night enveloping her discussion with Miles, "our short, stiff brush in the dark", is broken only by the white glitter of his teeth and eyes.

From this point onwards the story moves rapidly towards its climax. The progression of the imagery, recording the dark invasion, keeps pace. The governess notes: "The summer had turned, the summer had gone; the autumn had dropped upon Bly and blown out half our lights." She goes on to make an odd theatrical simile, perhaps provoked by some Jamesian recollection, perhaps intentionally located to support the dramatic construction of the whole: "The place, with its grey sky and withered garlands, its bared spaces and scattered dead leaves, was like a theatre after the performance —all strewn with crumpled playbills."

The climactic sequence with Miles, which marks the beginning of the governess's despair and the destruction of all hope, begins during a black evening when "a great wind was abroad" and the rain lashes at the windows. Again, the scene evoked is authentically Norwegian. The governess sits writing by the light of a dim lamp and then, uneasy, goes out into the darkness as before taking a smoking candle with her. She pauses at Miles's door and, to her surprise, finds that he is awake and apparently expecting her: he invites her in. His forced tone is "gaiety in the gloom", and after she enters, bearing her torch, she stands over him for a minute holding her light aloft. This scene—the dark room, the watchful little boy who never sleeps, the governess holding high her glow of freedom, beauty and innocence—catches in symbolic tableau the import of the whole nouvelle. When the governess sits down near Miles she puts the candle, as if for protection, a little way off. Her hope is to make him confess, reveal his secret for, as she remarks, "I'm in the dark." But she presses Miles too hard, forces the pace, and the answer to her appeal comes in the form of an "extraordinary blast and chill, a gust of frozen air and shake of the room as great as if, in the wild wind, the casement had crashed in." The invasion is manifest and, as in the third act of *Ghosts* when the doors are thrown open, the citadel has fallen. The governess, after Miles's shriek of terror, becomes "conscious of darkness" and then notes, with a shock, that her candle has gone out. Miles's glib, uneasy explanation, that he has blown it out, is both false and true. Literally, since it was set away from him, he could not have done it; symbolically, as the agent of darkness, he is in fact responsible. He has now become a "dark prodigy", capable of any evil: light has failed entirely. Later, when the governess and Mrs Grose go after Flora and retrieve her from the lakeside, it is noted that "the flicker had left her face"; she has become aged and ugly. The governess's deepest despair follows these two episodes, and she almost capitulates to the night. Her resignation is presented in a symbolic act:

> On the removal of the tea things I had blown out the candles and drawn my chair closer; I was conscious of a mortal coldness and felt as if I would never again be warm. So when he [Miles] appeared I was sitting in the glow with my thoughts.

All light, all hope, all beauty and innocence have faded, and the totally demoralised governess herself puts out the lights, even as Mrs Alving. All that remains is the dull glow from the hearth, dimly illuminating the gloom—making it even gloomier—like the embers from Captain Alving's charred memorial. The final, dreadful scene of the nouvelle, set inevitably in blackest night, yields only to the mocking light of dawn when Miles, like Oswald, has surrendered horribly to the dark.

This analysis does not of course exhaust the symbolic and imagistic elements in the tale. The theme of intrusion, which runs through the whole, is repeatedly imaged in a series of potent incidents. Here again the narrative process interacts skilfully with what becomes overt symbolism. Soon after Quint's first appearance, for example, the governess notes that "we had been, collectively, subject to an intrusion", and the pressing evil, which eventually smashes through the window of Miles's bedroom, or, like Miss Jessel, penetrates even to the schoolroom, the governess's own domain, enacts the process simultaneously in literal and symbolic terms. The force of the incident with Flora at the lakeside both derives from this persistent imagery and lends power to it. The episode records Miss Jessel's first appearance. Flora pretends not to see the apparition and then she

> picked up a small flat piece of wood, which happened to have in it a little hole that had evidently suggested to her the idea of sticking another fragment that might figure as a mast and make the thing a boat. This second morsel, as I watched, she was very markedly and intently attempting to tighten in its place. My apprehension of what she was doing sustained me so that after some seconds I felt I was ready for more. Then I again shifted my eyes—and faced what I had to face.

A multitude of associations, already carefully established, accrete at this instant to add intensity and horrid fascination to this little gesture. The controlling thought, as I have said, is that of intrusion, the stick forced into the wood: Miss Jessel's is an "alien" presence. At the same time there is a barely covert sexuality suggested, prepubescent genitalia, whose presence together with the faintest hint of incest runs through the tale. Finally, the model is associated with ships and the ocean—the lake has already, for the purpose of this scene, been christened the Sea of Azof—and all three are, throughout the story, exploited as images of the adult life for which the children are as yet so apparently ill-prepared. Flora's crude little boat mirrors, on this level, her premature aspiration to be a woman.

105

The invasion of the house by ghosts of blackest evil is itself a vast symbolic enactment of what is the central process in the tale, the corruption of young children from within. This is also, as I have shown, the central concern in *Ghosts*, and it is imaged in a similar manner. The intrusion of Rosenvold parallels the advancing moral illness in Oswald so that, symbolically speaking, the rising of the ghosts within the house implies their presence in Oswald's worm-eaten body. Into this set of ideas both Ibsen and James, as we have already seen, introduce the image of poison and the symbol of fever. In both *Ghosts* and *The Turn of the Screw* the miasma of the home is imaged as a moral poison which the children have innocently inhaled; and, having breathed it in, they sicken and so die. Before they do so, terrible fevers blight their young lives, a powerful symbol of the internal fetidness which mars the fair surface. *The Turn of the Screw*, like *Ghosts*, is a domestic drama.

Among the major pieces of evidence available to Edmund Wilson in his idiosyncratic reading of *The Turn of the Screw* is the curious confusion about the identities of Quint and the children's uncle which apparently exists only in the governess's fevered mind. His argument suggests that her sexual frustration, focused on her employer, expresses itself by creating a less exalted, and therefore more attainable figure ("Would he not have to stoop to love her?" asks Mr Wilson) who wears the uncle's clothes and edges excitingly and dangerously nearer and nearer. By way of reply, I would agree that there *is* a deliberate melding of identities between the two figures, but would argue that it is an externally imposed confusion written into the action in order to emphasise the nouvelle's moral point. Mr Wilson's insight is, I think, partially valid, but is also ultimately a distortion arising from his tendency to associate too closely quasi-independent elements in the plot: the sexual tension, which is integrated, as we have seen, with the concept of intrusion, and the complex symbol structure which necessarily posits a relation between its triunal parts. The verbal and visual connections establishing the links between Miss Jessel and the two men, in the governess's conversations with Mrs Grose and elsewhere, stress their moral affinities (especially those between Quint and the uncle) to create finally a compound figure which functions as a living, dangerous moral symbol. When we examine the text we see that the significant ambiguities relating to the figures of Quint and the uncle are by no means all the governess's:

> "The last governess? She was also young and pretty—almost as young and almost as pretty, Miss, even as you."
>
> "Ah, then, I hope her youth and her beauty helped her!" I recollect throwing off. "He seems to like us young and pretty!"
>
> "Oh, he *did*," Mrs Grose assented: "it was the way he liked everyone!" She had no sooner spoken indeed than she caught herself up. "I mean that's *his* way—the master's."
>
> I was struck. "But of whom did you speak first?"
>
> She looked blank, but she coloured. "Why, of *him*."
>
> "Of the master?"
>
> "Of who else?"

The rich ambiguities in this exchange compel a kind of intellectual doubletake. Mrs Grose *is* talking about Quint but she is also, we realise after a while, still talking about the uncle. The statements apply to both men. Quint's viciousness, hinted at for the first time in the phrase, "he seems to like us young and pretty", reflect back again upon his master. So closely do the two men resemble each other that the governess, when she first encounters Quint's ghost, mistakes his figure for the uncle's—another nicely ambiguous stroke which subsequently compels a second thought. Later we are told, on two separate occasions, that Quint was his employer's "own man", who stole his clothes and wore them when he was away. This not only images the synonymity of the two men, but suggests the uncle's continuing presence at Bly even in his absence. After Quint's death his spectral form continues to materialise in the master's vestments.

A further point, understressed in the nouvelle, it is true, but nevertheless there, is that morally speaking the uncle is almost as bad as his servant. Like Quint he is a sexual adventurer—one of the reasons why he cannot be bothered with the children—and he has a compelling power over women which he does not scruple to exploit. The governess is "not the first—and won't be the last" to be carried away by his good looks; she acknowledges herself that she cannot hope to be "the only one." Finally, the uncle is a liar. Throughout the story silence, as we have seen, is made to carry as heavy a moral load as language; perhaps even greater, since it is a part of the darkness. In as much as the governess has a weapon against the ghosts, it is her power to make the children speak, to bring their secret out into the light. Her failure to do so signals the collapse of hope. On at least three occasions, including the climactic final episode, she tries to make the children reveal their secret. "If [Miles] confesses, he's saved," she tells Mrs Grose. By the same token, earlier on, she suggests that there is a sinister quality in their silence about their period in Quint's care, as indeed there is; but the noteworthy point is that her employer is silent in the same way. He quite deliberately, we recognise in retrospect, goes out of his way to conceal the facts from her. His prevaricating omissions, and the children's, are equally sinister in the context of the tale.

This question, when probed, leads inescapably to the conclusion that James wished to identify the two men, and implicate them both, though perhaps not necessarily equally, in the moral contamination at Bly. The uncle's more-than-careless irresponsibility means that he is at least partly culpable for what happens; there is an oblique stress, in *The Turn of the Screw*, on the duties of parents or guardians. More significant, however, is the series of identifying clues we have just noted which establishes the nexus of moral and personal identities between the living uncle and the dead Quint. The purpose of this carefully plotted process, I have suggested, is the creation of a compound moral symbol (following the analogy of *Covering End*) which ramifies and, like the gloom, envelopes Bly.

I have made these points for two reasons. First, because we encounter a similar technical process at work in *Ghosts*; and second, because it will be part of my argument that the characters in each work correspond to one another, not only in the broad context of action and structure, but also in terms of particular moral and personal characteristics. The Quint/Uncle ghost-figure recalls the Alving/Engstrand presence; Miles recalls Oswald; Mrs Engstrand recalls Miss Jessel; Flora recalls Regina and the governess Mrs Alving. All these echoes are, of course, approximate; I must repeat my point that I am arguing for influence, not plagiarism. In the context of what we have already discovered about the thematic and technical affinities between *Ghosts* and *The Turn of the Screw*, however, they must be accorded considerable weight.

In what remains of this chapter I want finally to discuss the parallels that may be drawn between the two sets of ghosts and their prime male victims; critically speaking, these are the most fruitful and interesting. The others can, of course, be undertaken, and they are no less fascinating; but, for the argument to be wholly convincing, we would require to accumulate a great deal of detailed evidence which, once established, only confirms the fresh emphases emerging from the correspondences traced between the ghostly sets and Miles and Oswald. We will therefore confine our investigation to these two.

In *Ghosts* Ibsen effects a deliberate fusion of image between the crippled Engstrand and the ghost of Captain Alving. Mrs Engstrand's disgust at her husband's advances ("Let me go, Engstrand; let me be!") which Engstrand mimics in a piping tone, is a carefully inserted pre-echo in the first scene of what is later to become the central revelation in Mrs Alving's tale of her own unhappy marriage: "And then I heard—oh! it still sounds in my ears, so hateful and yet so ludicrous—I heard my own servant-maid whisper, 'Let me go, Mr Alving! Let me be.' " Engstrand and Alving are related, not only as lovers of Mrs Alving's maid, but as the fathers, in different senses, of her illegitimate daughter. A deliberate melding of identities occurs; both men are part of the same immoral process. Their pasts and futures are profoundly connected, not only through Regina and her mother, but also through the Orphanage and Manders. Engstrand, who finally goes off to raise a memorial "worthy of Captain Alving's memory" —a brothel—becomes the custodian of his reputation. His "sailor's home" is to be paid for by the Captain's money, that sullied fortune which Mrs Alving would not have Oswald touch because she wants him to inherit nothing from his father. The inheritance and its moral overtones thus becomes Engstrand's. His drunkenness, hypocrisy and sexual license make him a worthy recipient. In these qualities, and in his ability to protect his reputation despite all, he is the embodiment of the Captain's ghost. His viciousness is, like Alving's, associated with the sombre corrupting mists "out there"; his presence in the home, dripping with the devil's rain, is one of the manifestations of the spectre. The close and skilfully jointed interrelations between these two men, one living and one dead, operate on an illustrative and symbolic plane. Regina, in the first scene, advances from the conservatory and drives Engstrand away; but he returns again and again, like Alving's ghost. His club foot is a kind of moral equivalent to the Captain's venereal disease, an index of his corruption and acquired, similarly, through a lifetime of dissipation.

Engstrand, in a word, renders Alving credible. More important, however, is the conscious cross-cutting of moral and personal qualities which Ibsen effects to establish an independent and united compound symbol whose implications ramify throughout the action. The tight carpentry of its construction contributes to the power of the whole.

The component parts of Ibsen's symbol-compound can be compared directly with its equivalent in *The Turn of the Screw*. On one side stands Engstrand, the maid and Captain Alving, united in their viciousness and histories as a single force for moral evil. On the other, Jamesian side are Quint, Miss Jessel and the uncle, equally united and equally vicious. Their symbolic functions are the same. Containing each set of ghosts, as we have seen, is a bare, provincial, isolated house surrounded by a dismal and encroaching moral doom. The entire structure, representing the same qualities of illicit sexuality and lethal evil, exerts an inexorable pressure of corruption and corrosion which finally destroys the children at the centre of the tale.

In addition to these points of comparison there are some interesting parallels in detail between Peter Quint and Captain Alving: their lives, personalities and deaths contain remarkable affinities. Each was morally licentious yet personally magnetic, able to conceal from their public worlds much of their sensual hypocrisy and indulgence. Further, Quint's immorality, like Alving's, is imaged in his imperfect health, and there is even the slight hint, not followed up, that his fatal disease was, like the Captain's, venereal. At Quint's inquest, the governess notes, his drunkenness, the darkness and an icy slope "accounted for much" of the mystery surrounding his unexplained death; but "there had been matters in his life—strange passages and perils, secret disorders, vices more than suspected—that would have accounted for a great deal more."

Earlier I touched on the possibility that James's conception of Quint's apparition may have been related in some way to the Stranger who haunts Ellida and her family in *The Lady from the*

Sea. There are many points of contact between the two figures but the most interesting, for our purposes, other than the fact that they are both emblematic ghosts which are allowed to appear before the audience, are the unique physical characteristics which they share. Ibsen's mysterious Stranger is notable for his striking red hair and beard, one of the few characters in his work to be so endowed. Peter Quint (who, it will be remembered, "looks like an actor") is also red-headed and bewhiskered, and in addition to this perhaps significant detail shares the Stranger's compelling, staring, glaring eyes—eyes which command submission and induce fear. On the occasion of his first visitation, for instance, he stares fixedly at the governess and "even as he turned away [he] still markedly fixed me." During his second appearance he "stared into my face" before glaring about the room. His terrible eyes reveal that he has come to "get" someone. Finally, at the end of the nouvelle, he repeatedly "glares" through the window, endeavouring to summon Miles by the force of his gaze.

These staring, frightening and compelling eyes are, apart from his red hair, also the Stranger's most remarkable physical quality. Throughout *The Lady from the Sea* his eyes repeatedly "stare", "glare" and "summon", revealing his intention to "get" Ellida and carry her away. Like Quint, the Stranger makes his power felt by simply appearing; he says nothing. During his ghostly visitations he does nothing but stand outside and watch. His power over Ellida stems from his capacity to simultaneously "allure and affright"—a phrase which, although James does not use it, nicely describes Quint's power over Miles. A final detail which may be significant in this context is the fact that Ibsen's red-haired Stranger is described as a "Quaen"—from Finmark. If the correspondences between the two ghosts are more than coincidental, then it is just possible that this may have suggested Quint's odd name to Henry James. Thus the red-haired, staring, terrifying presence of *The Turn of the Screw*, a figure who reminds the governess of an actor, may perhaps have been prompted by some Jamesian recollection of a production of *The Lady from the Sea*. The play was in fact premièred in London within a few weeks of Elizabeth Robins's *Hedda Gabler* and, although there is no record of James having attended this production, or any other, it is quite likely that his intense interest in Ibsen at this time would have encouraged him to go. At all events we know from his reference to the play in his *Hedda Gabler* review, published in the following month, that it was among the first Ibsens he read.

My main point so far has been that Ibsen's *gengangere* and James's ghosts share too many characteristics—structural, in terms of the action, and personal—for facile dismissal as coincidence. Their affiliations, as an extension of the point, touch their victims too. We have already noted some of the parallels between Miles and Oswald—their primacy as prey, the nature of their corruption and the fevers which image the pestilence. But more significant, perhaps, is the symbolic function, in terms of the broad ethical argument, to which each child is put. Oswald, as an emblem of inner rottenness, expresses in its highest valency (the phrase is Francis Fergusson's) the complex portrayal of apparent health and inward decay which runs through the play. His representative role is defined soon after his first entrance when Mrs Alving, "beaming with delight", exclaims, "I know one who has kept both his inner and outer self unharmed. Just look at him Mr Manders." His decline into chaos from this point keeps pace with the escalating presence of the ghosts throughout, his illness ultimately a symbol of their victory. Rosenvold and Oswald, at the end, become a symbolic unit.

James makes similar emblematic use of Miles, and in strikingly similar terms. When he first enters, having been inexplicably dismissed from school, the governess finds it impossible to believe the implicit charge that he has corrupted the others. Curiously re-echoing Mrs Alving's words, she exclaims: "It doesn't live an instant. My dear woman, *look* at him!" Miles's beauty and apparent health, like Oswald's, belie his real condition. From this point onwards the governess discovers with increasing horror that he is *vermoulu*, like the Alvings, to the core. As in *Ghosts* the corrupting pressure of the pestilential spectres keeps pace with the advancing illness; and in the final moments Miles's fever represents their triumph. Again the house and the boy have become symbolically united.

A major part of the horror in both pieces is the unnatural old age which besets the children as a consequence of their contact with the demons. As the final act of *Ghosts* approaches Oswald degenerates into a horrid mock of senility, and just before his final collapse he describes the "unutterably loathsome" condition of a premature and prolonged second childhood, his terror of having to be "helpless like a little new-born baby, impotent, lost, hopeless, past all saving . . ." In *The Turn of the Screw* James exploits the same horror. The children age visibly as the plot evolves. At first Miles is simply precocious, so much so that the governess speculates at one point whether it might not have been sheer jealousy which caused his expulsion from school. Gradually he is shown to be much more mature than he should be; he has a frightening "secret precocity" and sexual awareness beyond his years. The governess slowly comes to realise that she is dealing with a child no longer, but a young adult. Likewise Flora, who participates in this symbolic/actual aging, becomes towards the story's end common, hard and ugly, an "old, old woman." Her real condition and her brother's is imaged in the "big ugly spray of withered fern" which she raises from the ground when the governess and Mrs Grose retrieve her from the lakeside after her meeting with Miss Jessel.

In neither *Ghosts* nor *The Turn of the Screw* is this process of premature aging a gratuitous piece of Gothicism introduced to provoke a delightful *frisson* of horror. On the contrary, a powerful dramatic point—the perversion of nature—is being made in both cases. The destruction of the children, itself a consequence of unnatural lust, is imaged in a premature old age which dehydrates youth and consumes its beauty. The tension and horror arising from this inversion of the natural order heightens in similar ways the sense of tragedy and loss which invests both pieces.

4

Han Er Deus Caritatis

The major phase in James's career is usually dated from 1901 with the completion of *The Ambassadors* and the publication of *The Sacred Fount*. *The Wings of the Dove* appeared in 1902, *The Ambassadors* in 1903 and *The Golden Bowl* in 1904. The narrative features of the final period have been frequently and accurately described: a heightened and involuted prose style, extension, a strong tragic undertow, the use of a small group of characters suspended, as it were, in a void; and, above all, the exploitation of a highly organised and integrated symbol structure. A consideration of these problems, particularly the last, will be my chief concern in this chapter.

Oscar Cargill, in his fine study of James's novels, records in passing his impression that there are important elements in both *The Ambassadors* and *The Golden Bowl* which may be attributable to the influence of Ibsen. Maggie and something of her predicament, he feels, suggest comparison with Nora Helmer, while Strether reminds him strongly of Rosmer. Both men are, for example, respected in their communities, both are the inheritors of a tradition of "discipline and honour", and both, finally, are emancipated by the subtle influence of a woman. Further, Cargill believes that Mrs Newsome's oppressive, unseen presence owes at least something to Ibsen's conception of Beata, the dead wife who haunts *Rosmersholm*. His conclusion is that "the play . . . must be considered one of the major sources of *The Ambassadors*." Unfortunately, however, Cargill does not extend his argument much beyond this suggestion and, as it stands, leaves me largely unconvinced. One hopes that at some stage he will develop his ideas. However, his remarks do bear out my own feeling that there are indeed strong traces of Ibsen to be found in all the major

115

writings of this period, and indicate the direction which a longer and more detailed consideration of this aspect of James's last period might follow. Throughout 1901–1905 and beyond, into the mysterious unfinished fictions such as *The Ivory Tower*, Ibsen continued to exert a vital formative pressure on his work. As I shall argue, the "major phase" was not the consequence of some abrupt technical departure as certain critics (Quentin Anderson for one) have viewed it, but was rather a logical continuation of everything he had been trying to do following the watersheds of 1891 and 1895. The seeds of his supreme fictions, in other words, were sown during the dramatic years.

In this chapter I shall be discussing primarily *The Wings of the Dove*. My reasons for selecting it for close analysis are varied, but principally they rest on what I hope will be the demonstrable belief that it was James's finest achievement, the greatest of his great novels and the work by which, ultimately, together with *The Portrait of a Lady*, he will be chiefly remembered. *The Wings of the Dove* combines in nice proportion linguistic tensility and invention, narrative power, vivid dramatic portraiture and action, and a tragic vision unmatched in English fiction since *Middlemarch*.

But secondly, I hope in passing to be able to counter in some measure that formidable school of criticism (again, resting its case on the representativeness of *The Wings of the Dove*) which persists in attributing the richness of the final harvest to the continuing impact of an American literary tradition on James's work; and in particular to the specific allegorical example of Hawthorne. According to this view the American Henry James, far from cutting himself off from the soil of his native New England, became indeed a Hawthornian allegorist after 1900, producing novels and tales which in structure and detail may be related profoundly to such feeble fictions as, for example, *The Marble Faun*.

In arguing for the European or Scandinavian Henry James, however, I don't want to suggest that I believe him to have been wholly unaffected by writers such as Hawthorne. James was a man peculiarly responsive to the works of others; as Elizabeth Robins recorded:

> Despair would settle on him when he recalled the gift of a book from this or that English novelist. He positively could not, he said,

read anything, now [1895], for the sake of the story. He had "lost his innocence." If a book interested him he wanted to rewrite it.

This was characteristic of his creative personality throughout his life and many fine critics, including James himself, have indicated how in his early years he borrowed from or used directly the work of other writers: Flaubert, for example, or George Eliot. Equally, Marius Bewley has shown conclusively that in early and middle period novels such as *Roderick Hudson* and *The Bostonians*, Hawthorne decisively affected important elements of characterisation or plot; and that in some of the later fiction, for instance *The Wings of the Dove*, aspects of the imagery are of a highly derivative nature. Where Bewley goes wrong, however, as I am going to prove, is in suggesting that the manner of James's later imagery follows its Hawthornesque source; that, according to Quentin Anderson's argument, during his major period James indeed became an allegorist and that therefore the novels of 1900–1905 should be read as vast metaphysical statements of his father's Swedenborgian mysticism.

I do feel it is necessary to dwell for a little on this point since we must, as it were, get the mixture right if we are finally to see the late fictions in their proper perspective. The Bewley-Anderson thesis has hardened somewhat into critical orthodoxy. My argument is that James was unquestionably influenced by Hawthorne, about whom he wrote with intelligence repeatedly, but not the Hawthorne of the allegories. What he admired was Hawthorne's sense of evil and moral transgression, and his ability to communicate it; but he was never happy about his use of allegory, which he dismissed as "one of the lighter exercises of the imagination." Hawthorne's repeated excursions in this direction, said James, occasionally put him in the utmost peril of "crossing the line that separates the sublime from its intimate neighbour." And elsewhere he stated flatly: "Many excellent judges, I know, delight in symbols and correspondences, in seeing a story told as if it were another and very different story. I frankly confess that I have as a general thing but little enjoyment of it and that it has never seemed to me to be, as it were, a first-rate literary form." James learnt a lot from Hawthorne, but it was never narrative technique. It was Ibsen, and Ibsen alone, who, after 1895, taught him how to exploit Hawthorne's Puritanist faculty for dealing with "moral

117

anxiety" and the "restless individual conscience" within the framework of Realist fiction. A close reading of the imagery and symbolism in *The Wings of the Dove*, which I will undertake presently, will put this point beyond dispute.

In the autumn of 1894, just as the ill-fated *Guy Domville* was going into production, Henry James made his first notebook entries for *The Wings of the Dove*. Inevitably, such were his interests and ambitions at the time, he viewed his *donnée* through his dramatic rather than his novelistic spectacles. And as we can see from his notes, he was still looking for that Ibsenic role which would suit Elizabeth Robins, and which he had been promising for months (in his guise as the English Ibsen) to create for her: "I seem to get almost a little 3-act play—with the main part for a young actress. I get, at any rate, a distinct and rather melodramatic *action*, don't I? *Voyons un peu.*"

Three months later, in the discontented winter of his theatrical failure, he took up the idea again. This time it seemed there were no alternatives; the *donnée* was to become a short novel on the international theme for Henry Harper. But the histrionic possibilities were not far from James's mind even then, and he noted: "Dimly the little drama looms and looms; and clearly it will come to me at last." What did come to him that February morning, however, and within moments of this note, was the little click of perception, so eloquently recorded and movingly explored, that the dramatist's key might fit the novelist's lock. It was while working on *The Wings of the Dove* that James stumbled on the divine principle of the scenario—and all the consequent technical innovations it entailed.

The origins of the novel, then, are deep in James's theatrical experience, and are closely associated with his triumphant realisation that the "infinite little loss" of his West End humiliation might be converted into an "infinite little gain" for narrative success. The novel itself was completed during a period when James had fully assimilated the dramatic analogy, and consciously so; for as he acknowledged in his preface to *The Ambassadors*:

> The material for *The Ambassadors*, conforming in this respect exactly to that of *The Wings of the Dove*, published just before it, is taken absolutely for the stuff of drama; so that, availing myself of the opportunity given me by this edition for some prefatory remarks

on the latter work, I had mainly to make on its behalf the point of its scenic consistency. It disguises that virtue, in the oddest way in the world, by just *looking*, as we turn its pages, as little scenic as possible; but it sharply divides itself, just as the composition before us does, into the parts that prepare, that tend in fact to over-prepare, for scenes, and the parts, or otherwise into the scenes, that justify and crown the preparation. It may definitely be said, I think, that everything in it that is not scene (not, I of course mean, complete and functional scene, treating *all* the submitted matter, as by logical start, logical turn and logical finish) is discriminated preparation, is the fusion and synthesis of picture.

This is the aspect of *The Wings of the Dove* I want to turn to now, first in order to test James's claim against the evidence of the achieved work, and thus account for the decidedly odd way its dramaturgy *is* disguised; and secondly, in order to distinguish his use of the theatrical metaphor at this time from his use of it during the immediate post-theatre period. Obviously there is a difference both in magnitude and kind between *The Wings of the Dove* and, say, *The Other House*; and if we are to argue, as I do, that each issued logically from the same pen and exists in the same stylistic continuum, some close analysis is clearly necessary. I want to be able to justify my insistence on the essential continuity of James's work after 1891, not only because it seems clear to me that this is the case, but also because James himself was in no doubt about it.

The sheer magnitude and weight of the major phase novels mark them off from their immediate predecessors, those crisply-drawn works which followed from James's resolution never to write another long fiction like *The Tragic Muse*. Extension characterises Jamesian innovation after 1900; not a fresh decline into verbiage but, to express it in his own theatrical terminology, the evolution of the five-act novel. The three-act extended prompt-book is of the middle and late nineties; the five-act narrative prose tragedy emerges with the new century. Each of the major novels divides into five discreet blocs of action: *The Golden Bowl*, to take the clearest example, is in five Parts, each corresponding to an act, and the total structure is supported by a wealth of theatre imagery designed to reinforce the technical scaffolding. Thus as Part Fifth of the novel opens, for instance, we read that Maggie "felt not unlike some young woman of the theatre who, engaged for a minor part in the play and having mastered her cues with anxious effort, should find herself promoted to leading lady and expected to appear in every act of the five." In this and comparable other ways James points through his imagery to the novel's construction. And similarly, *The Wings of the Dove* is also in five acts, equally well supported by dramatic imagery. In its case, as we shall see, the novel's ten symmetrically arranged Books divide naturally into five tightly-structured units which contain the action and keep the plot moving. Each of these five units is built up of a series of controlled and plotted scenes constructed quite clearly on a dramatic analogy.

A distinction, however, which will become clearer as this chapter develops, must be drawn at this point between James's use of his dramatic metaphor before and after the technical watershed of 1899–1900. Prior to the experimental crisis of *The Sacred Fount*, which is quite distinct in this regard from *The Awkward Age*, James's use of the theatre analogy tended to be rather mechanical and slightly doctrinaire, as we have seen. The failures of such novels as *The Other House* can be attributed at least in part to his determination to push the technical analogy as far as it could go, and the result, especially in the case I have just mentioned, is forced dialogue, heavy reliance on coincidence and an excessively mechanical plot. After 1900, however, James's use of the dramatic model in his fiction was marked by a greater flexibility and selectivity. Although he retained the tautness of structure and action which the scenic form and scenario method conferred, he allowed himself greater freedom when confronting problems of dialogue, characterisation and scenic shape. Thus although the vital factor remained the analogy of act and scene, the proscenium arch framing his moving canvasses, it would be wrong to expect to find that in these final novels each chapter contains its self-sufficient scene. This was one of James's departures from his earlier use of the idea. The pulsation of crises, experienced in the great scenes of a novel like *The Wings of the Dove*, is far slower than the rapid chapter-by-chapter presentation of *The Other House* and some of the other early play-novels and tales.

This introduces a point that needs stressing. In *The Wings of the Dove, The Golden Bowl, The Ambassadors* and *The Sacred Fount,* James used extensively and to great effect the technique of scenic disguise which he evolved, as we have seen, while writing *The Spoils of Poynton.* As I argued in the second chapter, this device involves the simple fragmentation of a single theatrical sequence, usually in dialogue form, into separate interviews divided from each other by a brief, discursive paragraph or elementary phrase suggesting that time and locality have changed. What James actually achieves is a single scene, "treating *all* the submitted matter, as by logical start, logical turn and logical finish", through a simple time-dislocation which suggests that it took place over an extended period. By eschewing the unity of time James achieved the unity of form.

A useful instance of this technique in action in *The Wings of the Dove,* representative of the kind of narrative tautness he was able to achieve in his final phase, is the sequence in which Milly and Susan Shepherd, early in the novel, discuss the nature of the relationship between Merton Densher and Kate Croy. It begins with Susan's anxiously innocent query, has Kate ever mentioned Densher to Milly? Milly makes the commonsense reply: of course not; why should she? What is there, or what should there be, between her and Merton? Susan's reply is a dark hint that there may be some significance in Kate's silence—as of course we, as readers, know there is. But at this point the scene is ostensibly broken off, though immediately it continues when "later on, late the same evening" during "a midnight conference" the conversation is renewed. Milly now reveals that so far as Kate's sister Marian is concerned (a disturbing fact in the context of Susan's questions) Densher's relative poverty constitutes a serious potential threat to the future welfare of the Croy family. At the same time—Milly and Susan hurry over the implications of this as by a mutual complicity—he is an able person who should get on in the world and he appears to be well liked by Mrs Lowder. Again the scene apparently ends here, but James adds: "Yet the matter was not left so, that night, between them, albeit neither perhaps could afterwards have said which had first come back to it." Thus the conversation "freshly flickers up" between the two women, and in the ensuing exchange it is drawn to its logical close. The emergent point is that there is a vague and undefined tension between Milly and Kate over Merton, although, so far as Milly knows, he is in love with neither of them and is not committed in any way. Her task, it appears, is nevertheless to get to him before Kate does in order to warn him not to reveal that they have met previously. This would free him—so both she and Susan rationalise it—from having to make any overt choice between herself and Kate.

It is obvious that despite the fact that these exchanges are located in varying places and times, they add up in conjunction to a single sequence from which all irrelevancies have been removed. Thus James himself defined 'scene.' Further, his manner here has its advantages over a staged dialogue. The action continues to move—a kind of narrative equivalent to the producer's blocking—and, by the persistence of the subject over an evening, shows that it is a principal thought in the minds of both women.

The technique of scenic disguise has other advantages too, and James exploits them to the full. Especially valuable is the buoyancy of movement which it confers, the brilliantly simple way in which it resolves the central difficulty of contriving convenient or necessary entrances and exits. Again an early scene contains a striking example of James's use of it in action. It opens with Mrs Lowder's request that Milly should try to discover from Kate whether Densher is back in London. James, in this scene, is beginning to integrate the fact of Milly's illness with the plight of Merton and Kate as sketched out in the Prologue. At the same time he begins to confirm our growing suspicion, aroused by Milly's curious reasoning in the sequence with Mrs Stringham we have just discussed, that she is herself in love with Densher. The situation he creates is described in a vivid theatrical image as "an occasion, in the quiet lamplight", which had "the quality of a rough rehearsal for the possible big drama." It is one of those apparently casual references which, as in *The Golden Bowl*, support and justify the technical mould into which he has poured the whole novel.

At this point Kate enters. It's a beautifully timed entry and splendid in its theatricality: the protagonist under intense discussion enters at the right moment. But it is also an appearance which James, in *The Other House* or *Covering End*, would have had to justify—within the laws of coincidence and convenience—by recourse to extended authorial apology or ingenuity. And then there is the problem of Mrs Lowder—how is she to be removed without stretching the credulity of the reader? James's technical skill, his simple device of scenic disguise, resolves in a stroke all these difficulties. The encounter, he suggests, takes place some time after Milly's discussion with Aunt Maud. Thus Mrs Lowder is quietly and effortlessly removed, and Kate is put in her place. Scenic unity is maintained and the action continues without a hitch.

Milly sets out to discover from Kate what her attitude is to Merton Densher. And although she does not succeed, the exchanges between the two women in this scene are central. Kate, hard-pressed by Milly for the first time, reveals many of those Hedda-like qualities which we will discuss in more detail presently: bright perversity, astounding frankness, ironic aggression and duplicity. She begins to establish her intellectual and personal ascendancy, while Milly gently asserts her moral innocence. In the course of this scene two of the novel's major images are cast for the first time: Milly the Dove and Kate the Panther, with Mrs. Lowder the bird of prey circling nearby. At the end of this exchange the action continues rationally: Aunt Maud enters to find out from Milly whether or not "it had all gone beautifully." Milly's reply is an answer to the question framed in the first part of the scene, ostensibly some days previously but in reality immediately prior to Kate's entrance: "I don't *think*, dear lady, he's here." Then, "with the new day", Milly goes off to the National Gallery to avoid Sir Luke Strett—and to bump into Kate and Merton.

James scholars have so often and so unanimously agreed that *The Wings of the Dove* is about Minnie Temple that one hesitates to differ. There is, after all, strong biographical evidence to support the accepted reading, and we have James's own repeated testimony in preface, notebook and autobiography that he sought in this novel to exorcise her ghost, thinly disguised as Milly Theale, "by wrapping it . . . in the beauty and dignity of art." Nevertheless, it seems to me that if we trust the tale rather than the teller, we find that it deals somewhat less with Milly than most readings have suggested. This is of course not to deny that she is one of its central figures, albeit completely passive, or that she is the source of the complex and beautiful imagery celebrated in the title. Neither, furthermore, do I want to deny that she was modelled to some extent on James's memory of his cousin. This simple biographical fact, however, has distorted our view of the plot so that we have forgotten that it does not deal principally with Milly Theale at all, but is of course about Kate Croy, that strange and complicated heroine with whom James begins and with whom he ends; whose actions form the basis of the novel's central episodes; and whose state of mind and soul and moral evolution or stagnation are its chief concerns. The novel's first reviewers, men who did not have James's interposing preface between themselves and the text, were under no misapprehension about the centrality of Kate. Oliver Elton, for example, who wrote perhaps the best of its early appreciations (*Quarterly*, October, 1903), was unequivocal in his analysis: it was upon Kate, "the arch-conspirator", he noted, that James bent "his intensest and finest light"; for it is she, by the end of the novel, who is "the sufferer, the protagonist, foiled by forces beyond her scope, yet holding firm, and remaining, in her own style, noble."

Something happened to this novel between conception and execution. To place James's initial notebook entries beside the achieved work is to become aware of the great gap between 1894 and 1902. The two pieces of writing are barely recognisable as referring to the same thing. James begins with Milly but ends with Kate. Increasingly her plight and personality came to dominate his interest until, by the time the novel was finished, this was the story's main concern. Milly's fate was poignant, even tragic; but, in the final analysis, secondary.

The explanation for this shift, I would suggest, lies partly in his continued interest in Ibsen and his achievement, and partly in the fact that the novel failed in serialisation. Taking the second point first, we know that *The Wings of the Dove* grew in length and complexity after it had been turned down by an American periodical: when James felt, that is to say, more free to develop its implications. As he recorded in a letter to H. G. Wells:

> [Joseph] Conrad saw a shorter [rough statement] of *The Wings of the D.*—also well enough in its way, but only half as long and proportionately less developed. *That* had been prepared so that the book might be serialised in another American periodical (what

secrets and shames I reveal to you!) and the thing (the book) was then written, the subject treated, on a more free and independent scale.

We may surmise that the original draft (now lost) catered largely for an American audience and, following James's early formulations, told the tragic tale of an American millionairess in Europe. Later, when James felt liberated from the restrictions of serialisation and, so far as audience was concerned, inclined to cater only for himself and the coterie who read his novels, the Ibsen in him once again asserted itself. In particular, as I shall presently seek to show, *Hedda Gabler* and *John Gabriel Borkman* (for which James had the highest regard) played a crucial part in his freer and more independent treatment of its subject. *The Wings of the Dove*, like these two plays of Ibsen's, and like most of James's fiction after 1891, depicts a complex personality in crisis. It is, in the words he used to describe *Hedda Gabler*, "the study of an exasperated woman", one who is "infinitely perverse" and "perfectly ill-regulated." I will, of course, be coming back to all of these points; but first I want to show how James expressed in scenic terms his vision of this later Hedda, and of her father, Lionel Croy, who owes so much to John Gabriel himself. In form and spirit the novel follows Ibsen.

The first scene establishes carefully and unambiguously the major points which link Kate to Hedda and Lionel to John Gabriel: that their perverse and complex personalities prevent an adequate adjustment to the environment in which they find themselves. Scene 1 plunges us straight into the crisis: the curtain rises. What is revealed is a set of Ibsenic gloom and middle-class vulgarity expressed in seedy furnishings and shabby coverlets. In this context, and in contrast with the urban squalor of the room, is Kate Croy, discovered in a characteristic posture. She is waiting. It is a vignette, a tableau, which establishes her graphically in the mind: a visual objective correlative. Further, as Ian Watt has noted, James's first words, "She waited", point clearly to his dramatic intent: the notion of a woman waiting antecedes the knowledge of who she is.

The vulgar little room itself constitutes a statement in the Ibsen manner. Lionel Croy's moral turpitude, of which we shall say more presently, is reflected in the environment he creates about himself: his furnishings, as he does, evoke "the failure of fortune and honour." Kate, although we do not realise it until later, is in fact in her appropriate setting. The dissonances of her personality, as they emerge, complicate the predicament of her maladjustment by producing the violent physical and moral wavering between Mrs Lowder's parvenu splendour and Lionel's depressing sordidity which is the overall patterning of the novel. This movement follows, I think significantly, that of *Hedda Gabler*: Hedda moves outwards and away from her father in the first part of the play, but returns to his environment and values (never having really abandoned them, we finally realise) at the end.

James dramatises vividly the ethos and quality of Kate's moral and material heritage in this first scene, and also takes the opportunity to provide a rationale for her future scheming. Her attachment to Lionel is primary and, as her behaviour at the end of the novel shows, constitutes her major loyalty. She goes away from this initial encounter with him with a motive and an ethical context: axioms of the plot to which James, as we shall see, attached great importance.

The second scene of the play underscores firmly the points made in the first: James emphasises Kate's dubious moral legacy and drab environmental origins. She is still the centre of the action, but now seen with her depressed and depressing sister, Marian, whose faded vitality stresses the consequences of poverty, of disadvantageous marriage. Kate's immediate family is uniformly bankrupt, both financially and morally, though by one of the few fine impulses of which she is possessed, she is deeply attached by ties of loyalty and pride to its reputation and good name. In this scene, like a skilful dramatist, James mentions Densher and his relation to Kate for the first time—a preparatory stroke for the next sequence which shows the increasingly intriguing heroine with her lover for the first time.

Scene three is crucial. It draws together and restates in amplified form the major themes of the act and, as we later realise, of the drama itself: the facts of Kate's moral inheritance, the insistent presence of Lionel's dishonour, and the poverty which stands as a barrier between the two young people. It is a key moment, a pivotal scene, about which the rest of the action will gradually turn.

The fourth scene is an interview between Mrs Lowder and Merton Densher; their subject is of course Kate and his relationship with her. In passing, but not irrelevantly, James describes with care what is to be Kate's new and adoptive environment, a world which, in its squalid grandeur, is implicitly contrasted and compared with the first scene's squalid poverty. Maud's furnishings, like Lionel Croy's, exude an aura, a comment about their owner; and we are told that as Densher awaits her entrance he takes in "the message of her massive florid furniture, the immense expression of her signs and symbols." The function of this scene, apart from the conveyance of these messages, is to dramatise Aunt Maud's attitude and to make explicit her plans for Kate. Densher is to be accepted as a suitor on sufferance until somebody more suitable, which is to say wealthier, can be found.

The final scene of the act presents the last important axiom in Kate's drama. The consequences of Aunt Maud's inflexible hostility to Densher is secrecy; and with secrecy comes intensity. The two lovers pledge eternal loyalty to one another:

> Suddenly she said to him with extraordinary beauty: "I engage myself to you forever."
> The beauty was in everything, and he could have separated nothing—couldn't have thought of her face as distinct from the whole joy. Yet her face had a new light. "And I pledge you—I call God to witness!—every spark of my faith; I give you every drop of my life."

James is careful to emphasise the importance of this declaration:

> They had exchanged vows and tokens, sealed their rich compact, solemnized, so far as breathed words and murmured sounds and lighted eyes and clasped hands could do it, their agreement to belong only, and to belong tremendously, to each other. They were to leave the place accordingly an affianced couple . . .

The act concludes with Densher's convenient removal to the United States on an assignment for his newspaper. There, with equal convenience, he will meet Milly Theale, the Good Heroine, who is just about to enter this drama. The Prologue is complete.

In describing this act as a Prologue I have kept in mind James's critique of *Hedda Gabler* that "something might have been gained" by providing a context and a history for Hedda's subsequent behaviour; for this is precisely what he provides in the case of Kate Croy. If major elements of *The Wings of the Dove* were suggested, as I shall argue, by *Hedda Gabler*, then it would be entirely logical in the face of James's critique of the play to anticipate a Prologue in which the antecedents and explanations of Kate's subsequent actions are offered. The "blest" *Other House*, as we have noted, constituted a precedent and light to walk by in this regard, and indeed the affinities between that novel and *The Wings of the Dove* have been noticed by many critics. Kate's situation, personality and dramatic plight are at the heart of the first act; her maladjustment to her environment, both Lionel's and Maud's, is dramatised; her dishonoured inheritance and her devotion to her family are emphasised and emphasised again; and her secret love and its eternal quality are established as central facts in the plot. All these elements of the action, without which Kate would become indeed a veritable Hedda, are carefully delineated. And significantly enough they are all realised, as we have seen, in strictly scenic terms and in the course of an act of magnificent theatricality.

I have discussed the Prologue of this play-novel in some detail for two reasons. First, I wanted to emphasise the centrality of Kate, to make clear the point that Milly's appearance constitutes (so far as the action is concerned) a complication of *her* situation and not the other way round. To focus critical interest on Milly, as Leavis does in his dismissal of the book, is a distortion of the novel's impact. There is certainly a relation between the fates of the Good and Bad Heroines, and each suffers in her own way; but we should not lose sight of the fact that Kate is the keystone of the novel's arch.

Secondly, I wanted through this detailed analysis to show how James used his dramatic analogy in *The Wings of the Dove*. In a study of this length it would be both tedious and wasteful of space to continue in the same way through the entire novel; we have seen repeatedly how James exploited his new metaphor with regard to his earlier prose fictions, and it should be clear from this that he continued to do so even after his return to a more expansive form in 1900. What follows, therefore, is an abbreviated version of what could clearly be a much longer demonstration; and it is hoped that those readers interested in pursuing this aspect of the novel in more detail will consider the tables set out below in conjunction with the close analysis of the first act we have just completed, together with the fuller discussions of *The Spoils of Poynton* and *The Turn of the Screw* earlier in the book.

Act and Scene Structure in *The Wings of the Dove*.

ACT ONE: *Books one and two*

Scene 1: Kate and Lionel. Heredity. Motive and context.
Scene 2: Kate and Marian. Kate's future? Densher mentioned.
Scene 3: Densher and Kate. Their situation and its background.
Scene 4: Densher and Aunt Maud. Her implacable opposition.
Scene 5: Densher and Kate. Exit Densher, linked forever to Kate, for the U.S.A.

ACT TWO: *Books three and four*

Scene 1: Milly *en tableau* at the abyss edge.
Scene 2: Milly and Susan Shepherd. The link with Maud indicated.
Scene 3: The dinner at Lancaster Gate. Milly and Lord Mark.
Scene 4: Milly's soliloquy. Her reactions to the company and to Kate.
Scene 5: Milly and Susan discuss Kate and Merton. A "disguised" scene. (See discussion of this scene above).

ACT THREE: *Books five and six*

Scene 1: Milly and Maud. "You must stay."
Scene 2: The Matcham portrait scene. Milly and Lord Mark.
Scene 3: Milly and Kate before the portrait. A "disguised" scene; exit Kate; enter Sir Luke Strett; exit Sir Luke; re-enter Kate. Milly and Kate conclude the scene.
Scene 4: Milly and Sir Luke. He passes sentence on her.
Scene 5: Milly's soliloquy as she wanders in the park.
Scene 6: Milly and Kate. Kate's plan begins to form.
Scene 7: Milly and Mrs Lowder. "Is Densher back?" A "disguised" scene. (See discussion of this scene above.) Enter Kate: "You're a Dove." Exit Kate; re-enter Aunt Maud and Susan Shepherd. Exit Milly for the National Gallery (to avoid Sir Luke).
Scene 8: The National Gallery scene: Milly runs into Kate and Densher.
Scene 9: Kate and Densher afterwards.
Scene 10: The dinner scene. Milly too ill to attend.

Scene 11: Kate and Densher alone. She urges him to make up to Milly. Her full plan still undisclosed.

Scene 12: Densher goes to visit Milly. Exit Milly to change.

Scene 13: Enter Kate, and to her surprise finds Densher. The edge of her jealousy; Milly's sweet innocence begins to come between Kate and Merton.

ACT FOUR: Books seven and eight

Scene 1: Milly and Susan. They discuss Kate and Merton, and Milly's health.

Scene 2: Susan and Mrs Lowder: Milly discussed.

Scene 3: Milly and Susan: preparation for next scene.

Scene 4: Milly and Sir Luke. He encourages her to live, and to go away.

Scene 5: Three weeks later, in Venice. Milly and Lord Mark. The scene ends with the news of Densher's arrival.

Scene 6: Kate and Densher. The piazza scene when he invites her to his rooms.

Scene 7: Densher and Susan before dinner. Milly discussed.

Scene 8: The dinner. Milly, dazzling in white, outshines even Kate. The beginning of Milly's dying, and victory.

Scene 9: Densher and Kate. She urges him on. The scene ends with her promise to come to his rooms.

ACT FIVE: Books nine and ten

Scene 1: Milly and Merton. His tension at having to deceive her, and increasing fondness for her.

Scene 2: Densher's soliloquy as he waits in Venice. He catches a glimpse of Lord Mark.

Scene 3: Susan and Densher. Milly has turned her face to the wall. Susan tells of Lord Mark's visit.

Scene 4: Densher and Sir Luke Strett, who has come to see Milly.

Scene 5: London, three weeks later. Kate and Densher confronted; his suspicion that she has contrived to hurt Milly through Lord Mark. Kate's counter-accusation that he is in love with Milly. Enter Mrs Lowder who, "by the end of the week", discusses Milly with Densher. They already speak of her as though she were dead.

Scene 6: Kate and Densher. The deep rot in their relationship.

Scene 7: Densher meets Aunt Maud. He learns of Kate's return to her father and his environment. Milly's death at last.

Scene 8: Merton and Kate in her original environment. A "disguised" scene, including the script-burning episode, which runs through to the end. Milly's spirit triumphs, and the curtain immediately falls.

At the centre of *The Wings of the Dove*, as in *Hedda Gabler* and *John Gabriel Borkman*, we find a sexual triangle composed of personalities trapped in a situation not wholly of their own making. So far as the latter play is concerned, Ella Rentheim's poignant predicament, like Milly's, is made even more moving by the incurable disease which besets her and which lends pathetic urgency to everything she does. It is difficult not to feel that this wealthy, emotionally fecund, dying woman, who struggles with her sterile, vigorous and destitute sister for the soul of the man they both love, added something to James's conception of Milly Theale. But it is *Hedda Gabler* which is the main source for this novel. The tension between Kate and Milly over Densher is the mainspring of the action, the situation which brings Kate's complex and neurotic personality to its crisis. The tragic situation which ensues is doubly ironic for Kate, since her triumphant opponent is hardly her intellectual equal: an irony directly echoed in Hedda's despair. Kate's role, like Hedda's, is that of an apparently coolly calculating aggressor; Milly, on the other hand (her last name may, incidentally, owe something to Thea), is on the defensive. She is only half aware of the bitter struggle in which she is engaged; her strength, like Mrs Elvsted's, lies in her innocence and simple devotion. Primary to the moral and personal collisions in both pieces is the tension between the driving, passionate ambition of a beautiful, talented but perverse young woman, and the fecund emotional power of a less complex, but no less attractive, rival. She, the beautiful evil heroine, covets her opponent's power, and in trying to possess it learns how to destroy it—or so she believes. Between the two women, the subject of their unspoken struggle, is an attractive but weak young man whose loyalties and emotional commitments move gradually into the foreground as the story unwinds. The struggle becomes a battle for his soul. The fair-haired Good Heroine defeats her darker-haired rival; but she, the loser, learns to kill in a last, destructive gesture. In *Hedda Gabler* she destroys the young man and the "child" which is the product of his fruitful union with the other; in *The Wings of the Dove* she encompasses the destruction of the young woman herself. In neither case, however, does this violence bring victory; it merely compounds defeat. In *Hedda Gabler* Thea's power is paradoxically increased: she simply absorbs Tesman and inspires him to try to recreate Lövborg's great work. In *The Wings of the Dove* Kate's action ensures, at least for Densher, the immortality of Milly; she becomes a martyr and a saint. Defeated thus on every side, the Bad Heroine is faced with defiance or compromise. In both cases she chooses neither: she simply opts out. Hedda kills herself; Kate elects self-exile. Both gestures are final, irrevocable, deliberate commitments to oblivion. Kate embraces social death and, as Lionel's remorse suggests, perpetual self-torment. Hedda selects a grotesque exit which leaves everyone around her stunned. The two actions, though unlike in degree, resemble each other in decision and kind.

But Kate Croy, let it be conceded immediately, is not simply a recreation of Hedda Gabler. She is not, to put it another way, Rose Armiger. Nevertheless, there are sufficient parallels and echoes to suggest that Ibsen's cold-eyed heroine may not have been far from James's mind when he created her; or, again, to put it the other way, Kate and Rose have too much in common to permit us to overlook their common ancestry.

Located in the early stages of the novel is an important pointer to Ibsen's continued exemplary presence in James's creative mind after 1900. His theory of moral consanguinity—that ethical behaviour is the consequence of genetics and early environment—was, as we have seen, a regular feature of James's work after he first encountered it. He based upon it at least one play, *The Reprobate*, and exploited it to some extent in four others: *The Saloon*, *Guy Domville*, *Summersoft* and *The High Bid*. In the years after 1891 he returned to it repeatedly in novels and tales as well: *Owen Wingrave*, *Covering End* and, as we saw in the last chapter, *The Turn of the Screw*. *What Maisie Knew* and *The Awkward Age* may also be considered to some extent as examinations of the proposition. In 1901–2 he turned to it again, this time to provide, as I suggested in my discussion of the Prologue to *The Wings of the Dove*, an antecedent explanation for Kate Croy's strange and morally ambiguous behaviour. Ibsen's notions of ethical inheritance underlie the plot of *The Wings of the Dove*, and provide one of the keys to our understanding of its heroine's complex personality.

Lionel Croy's warped personality and social dishonour, the dominating factors in Kate's upbringing, are also part of the moral legacy which he bequeaths to his child: James offers this fact by way of explanation and also, to some extent, by way of exoneration. She is simply, like Hedda Gabler, her father's daughter:

> "Well then," said Kate, "he has done some particular thing. It's known. Only, thank God, not to us. But it has been the end of him. *You* could doubtless find out with a little trouble. You can ask about London."
>
> Densher for a moment said nothing; but the next moment he made it up. "I wouldn't find out for the world, and I'd rather lose my tongue than put a question."
>
> "And yet it's part of me," said Kate.
>
> "A part of you?"
>
> "My father's dishonour." Then she sounded for him, more deeply than ever yet, her note of proud, still pessimism. "How can such a thing as that not be the great thing in one's life?"

Lionel's disgrace is *the* thing Kate is; the burden she must carry, as Milly bears her money, like a pile, on her back. The contrasting inheritances which neither girl can avoid are counterposed in striking terms. Kate's indigent malignancy—and the two are, like wealth and moral beauty, linked as a symbol in the novel—has been inherited or at least acquired during early childhood, like Milly's affluent gentleness. In his preface to the 1907 edition of the novel James lamented the exigencies of space and time which had prevented him from sufficiently emphasising this point:

> The image of [Kate's] so compromised and compromising father was all effectively to have pervaded her life, was in a certain particular way to have tampered with her spring; by which I mean that the shame and the irritation, and the depression, the general poisonous influence of him, were to have *show*n, with a truth beyond the compass even of one's own most emphasised "word of honour" for it, to do these things.

It is not coincidental, in my judgment, that in this passage James selects two images—the poisoned stream and the mephitic ethos—which not only recall Ibsen but which look back to his own use of Ibsen's ideas. The image of the tainted spring, it will be remembered, was used in connection with Paul Doubleday and his moral relation to his mother; the miasma of evil invested Bly. It might also be interesting in this connection to note that over the page James refers to Lionel as a "damning apparition." In addition we should recall that he had the greatest admiration for the "splendid" *John Gabriel Borkman,* and this seems to have found expression, not only in those echoes of the play which we have already noted, but in the figure of Lionel Croy. Like John Gabriel, he is a man of worldly success who, through some terrible crime, is condemned in his last years to loneliness and social excommunication. Lionel's wicked deed is never revealed; all we learn is that he is someone "odious and vile", a man to whom "something or other happened that made him impossible. I mean impossible for the world at large first, and then little by little, for mother."

It is from the loins of this man that Kate Croy springs; to whom, in the first Book, she pledges undying loyalty, and to whom, in the last, she finally returns, guilty of an evil worthy of her name. Further, despite the several links with Ibsen's drama in general which this idea establishes, we need seek no further than *Hedda Gabler* itself for a precedent. James's attitude to the complex blood-moral relationship between father and daughter closely resembles Ibsen's conception of the consanguinity between Hedda and General Gabler. "The title of the play is *Hedda Gabler,*" Ibsen wrote to Moritz Prozor in 1890,

> My intention in giving it this name was to indicate that Hedda as a personality is to be regarded rather as her father's daughter than as her husband's wife.

Similarly, it was James's intention that Kate should be seen rather as her father's daughter than as Densher's lover. General Gabler is not, of course, Lionel Croy; but his style of life and violent personality, like Lionel's polluting evil, are both an anticipation of and a preparation for his daughter's destructive career. As Northam has observed of Hedda, "behind everything hangs the portrait of her father, the General, the social and hereditary force which dooms her to stultifying isolation." Kate's adventure, similarly, constitutes a sally from the grim paternal environment in which we first discover her. Later, in eventual defeat, she retreats to that world again, retiring like Ibsen's morbid heroine (again to quote Northam) "beaten, to a final refuge with her General father, the cause of her tragedy and its ultimate solution."

Kate's defining characteristic, the quality which puts her in the same category as Rose Armiger and Hedda Gabler, is her anti-heroic ambiguity. She is, like her predecessors, the corrupt protagonist of the action she dominates; like Rose a "Bad Heroine"— that ironically paradoxical type which James, working under the spell of *Hedda Gabler*, created for *The Other House*. Early in the novel he carefully delineates Kate's type, using terms which recall Hedda at every point:

> Kate knew what to think of her power thus to carry by storm; she saw herself as handsome, no doubt, but as hard, and felt herself as clever but as cold; and so much too perfectly ambitious besides, that it was a pity, for a quiet life, she couldn't settle to be either finely or stupidly indifferent. Her intelligence sometimes kept her still—too still—but her want of it was restless; so that she got the good, it seemed to her, of neither extreme.

The ambiguity which distinguishes the bad heroine provokes an ambivalent response on the part of those who encounter her. This was Hedda's remarkable quality, so far as James was concerned, when he first described her contradictory, perplexing personality: she was exposed to "a dozen different interpretations", and one could by no means dismiss her simply as either wholly wicked or disagreeable. She was complicated, strange, irreconcilable, infernal; sinuous, but graceful; various, but natural; capable of working on others and becoming a part of their history. A big personality; in a word, rather like Kate. And James, in *The Wings of the Dove*, went to great lengths to establish the fact of his heroine's parallel qualities. She is both devious and frank, passionate and cold, tender and brutal. The ambivalence of Densher's confused responses to her, carefully noted at almost every encounter, illustrates each of these points. During the crucial scene in which he slowly begins to comprehend the moral enormity of her crime, for example, he grips her shoulders and shakes her softly, "as if in expression of more mingled things, all difficult, than he could speak." In the New York edition, so as to emphasise Densher's conflicting emotions, James changed "difficult" to "different". Merton is torn between violence and gentleness, between hostility and worship—he holds her "hard", but shakes her "far from untenderly"—even hate and love. Finally, in confusion, he makes a simple gesture of submission. He does not kiss Kate; he merely "applied his lips to her cheek." At the centre of this relationship is something very like the quality of emotion binding Hedda to Lövborg.

These parallels can be extended further. The tender brutality which characterises Kate's attitude to Milly can be compared directly with the quality of Hedda's personal ascendancy over Thea. When at one point Hedda clasps her "passionately in her arms" Thea struggles to break free, crying "Let me go! Let me go! I'm afraid of you, Hedda!" Alone in the house at night with this tense and malignant personality, Thea senses her frustration and barely suppressed violence, and grows afraid. Similarly, when Kate in a moment of comparable jealousy and candour urges Milly to "drop us while you can", Milly

> tried to be amused so as not—it was too absurd—to be fairly frightened. Strange enough indeed—if not natural enough—that, late at night thus, in a mere mercenary house, with Susie away, a want of confidence should possess her. She recalled, with all the rest of it, the next day, piecing things together in the dawn, that she had felt herself alone with a creature who paced like a panther. That was a violent image, but it made her a little less ashamed of having been scared.

In her complex, intense and self-contradictory way, then, Kate appears closely to resemble Hedda. Further uniting the two women as types, however, is their joint capacity for passion without emotion, the quality which to some extent renders their behaviour intelligible. It is Kate's very shallowness which, in conjunction with her ambition and intelligence, enables her to conceive of a plan which views another human being as simply a substantial bank account. In the latter sections of the novel it is this same quality which allows her to perceive, quite accurately, that Milly's generosity to Densher is a challenge to herself which must be met. In one sense, therefore, Kate's capacity for cold passion, like

Hedda's, can be seen as a strength. Yet it is, at the same time, her greatest weakness, the factor which renders Milly's victory ultimately possible. The shocking thing about Kate's visit to Densher's rooms is not that she sleeps with him but the spirit in which she does so. Densher seeks a token of love but finds only cupidity: Kate goes to bed with him not from passion but from ambition. It is not that he finds this encounter unsatisfactory; far from it. But what he dimly begins to realise is that she was capable of viewing her virginity as something very like a saleable commodity: her most private world is subordinate to her ambition. In the same way, Hedda's emotionless, passionate greed, which we looked at in an earlier chapter, enables her to view both Lövborg's life and work, itself an expression of Thea's love and generosity, as both a challenge to be met and as a means to the gratification of her ego. And in the same way it is this same quality, in its negative form, which ensures her defeat at Thea's hands.

These points can perhaps best be illustrated by comparing two central episodes from either work. Kate's personal tension, like Hedda's, is based on frustrated aspiration, and is released in bursts of violent and irrational destructiveness. Hedda brings down Lövborg and destroys his manuscript; Kate encompasses Milly's death and burns her letter to Densher. The scene in which she does so images, in terms of motive and violence, her destruction of the dove, and invites immediate comparison with one of the most dramatic moments in *Hedda Gabler*:

> She had a last hesitation, but she presently broke it. "Trust me." Taking from him the sacred script, she held it a little, while her eyes again rested on those fine characters of Milly's which they had shortly before discussed. "To hold it", she brought out, "is to know."
>
> "Oh, I *know*," said Merton Densher.
>
> "Well then, if we both do—!" She had already turned to the fire, nearer to which she had moved, and with a quick gesture, had jerked the thing into the flame.

The effects for which James is reaching in this passage seem clearly enough related to the powerful third act finale of *Hedda Gabler*. Milly's letter represents for Kate, as Eilert's manuscript for Hedda, an opposing moral pressure which must be met and destroyed: it is the expression of another's love and tender devotion. The temptation and opportunity presented by the fire is too great, and with jealousy in her heart, and a momentary sense of triumph, she feeds the precious script to the flames. As Frederic Crews remarks, "It is an act of horrible jealousy. Kate sees that Milly is triumphantly *good*, and she cannot bear to compete with her for Densher's soul." This is an observation which also describes Hedda's emotions, and James's scene irresistibly evokes the Ibsenic moment. Laurence Holland, for instance, directly compares the two episodes, commenting that the scene in *The Wings of the Dove* has the same "terrifying power" as that in *Hedda Gabler*. Yet he does not go on to ask himself why James's scene should recall Ibsen's. In my judgment it does so only because throughout the novel Kate herself continually evokes Hedda; she is a matrix of responses and qualities profoundly Norwegian in origin and scope. James's own analysis of Hedda's motives, relating them to her complicated passions, is the true link between these two episodes.

The core of my argument, I said earlier, is that it was Ibsen who showed James how to use Hawthorne. By implication I am contesting the widely held view, resting on the twin supports of Marius Bewley's *The Complex Fate* and Quentin Anderson's *The American Henry James*, that the technical innovations of the major phase novels can be satisfactorily attributed to James's admiration of Hawthorne. My point is, however, that there is symbolism and symbolism; that while James may well have taken some specific image from Hawthorne, the manner in which he developed it was far from Hawthornesque and in no sense allegoric. What I want to examine now, and in conclusion as it were, is the process of James's imagery and symbolism in *The Wings of the Dove*, and thus implicitly in all the late novels, illustrating in a concrete way what I take to be the errors of Bewley's analysis. My final point is that the base line of late Jamesian innovation must be drawn in 1891, during the dramatic years, and not after 1900; the technical continuity of all James's post-Ibsen fiction has to be clearly established.

It was her nature, once for all—a nature that reminded Mrs Stringham of the term always used in the newspapers about the great new steamers, the inordinate number of "feet of water" they drew: so and if, in your little boat, you had chosen to hover and approach, you had but yourself to thank, when once motion was started, for the way the draught pulled you. Milly drew the feet of water, and odd though it might seem that a lonely girl, who was not robust and who hated sound and show, should stir the stream like a leviathan, her companion floated off with a sense of rocking violently at her side.

Commenting on this passage Bewley makes the extraordinary assertion that the metaphor it contains is "completely inappropriate"; that in using it James has laid himself open to the charge of "unsteadiness of imagery". Doves, he says, should not be imaged as ships. A more rigorous analysis of the novel, however, and especially of those passages relating to Milly Theale, reveals that on the contrary ocean and water images are more consistently employed than any other. Milly is characteristically pictured as surrounded by a sinister rising tide, identified alternately with Kate and her illness, which finally engulfs her. Venice, and not the Dove, is the novel's dominating central symbol.

When we first encounter Milly in Book Third she is perched precariously over a mighty abyss. Her journey to this precipice evokes in strikingly Ibsenic terms her upward struggle throughout the book—I am thinking here of the ascensions in such plays as *Brand, John Gabriel Borkman* and *When We Dead Awaken*. It is significant that during an important scene with Susan she prefers ignorance to knowledge, the abyss to the sea: "Don't tell me that—in this for instance—there are not abysses. I want abysses." Gradually, in terms of the imagery, the gaping chasm of her life fills with the waters of her impending doom until, trapped in the topmost tower of her Venetian palace (she never descends) she is engulfed. At this point her spirit, liberated, soars on its wings above the encroaching waves.

Milly is a later Ishmael, twice imaged as the survivor of a general shipwreck in which all have drowned save herself. When explaining to Sir Luke Strett, her physician, that she has no immediate family, she uses the image explicitly. Later Densher uses it as well:

"She affects one, I should say, as a creature saved from a shipwreck. Such a creature may surely, in these days, on a doctrine of chances, go to sea again with confidence. She has *had* her wreck—she has met her adventure."

139

"Oh, I grant you her wreck!"—Kate was all response so far. "But do let her have still her adventures. There are wrecks that are not adventures."

"Well—if there also be adventures that are not wrecks!"

At this point, a moment in the novel when important equations are being established, Kate is subtly identified with the death-dealing oceanic surge in which Milly is to be wrecked for the last time. In the context of our analysis we can see, perhaps a little too sharply, how James contrives to plant his conceit. "I'm a brute about illness," Kate tells Densher; "I hate it. It's as well for you, my dear, that you're as sound as a bell." Densher laughingly replies: "Thank you! It's rather good then for yourself too that you're as strong as the sea."

As soon as Milly descends from the high mountain ledge on which we first discover her she is plunged into perilous watery depths. The image, overtly simple, is deployed with great complexity, and James takes great care to prepare for it in advance: to give it credence, as it were. Densher's early "plunge into London", for instance, his initiation into society, is accomplished after a "descent . . . through zones of air that had left their ruffle on his wings." Finally he floats calmly and successfully on its surface. But Milly's plunge leaves her winded, and she immediately begins to sink. At Mrs Lowder's dinner party, the first social engagement of her stay, "words reached her from here and there like plashes of a slow thick tide", while Aunt Maud herself, formidably equipped for survival, "called at subjects as if they were islets in an archipelago." A little later, after a pause, she resumes "with a splash of her screw her cruise among the islands."

But Milly and Susan are completely out of their depth. Afterwards both are "slightly gasping" and "their immediate lesson, accordingly, was that they just had been caught up by the incalculable strength of a wave that was actually holding them aloft and that would naturally dash them wherever it liked." They are suspended precariously in a treacherously complacent ocean, limitless in its powers and mysterious in its vagaries, which might at any moment overwhelm them. James makes the point with firm insistence:

> The sense was constant for [Mrs Stringham] that their relation was as if afloat, like some island of the south, in a great warm sea

140

that made, for every conceivable chance, a margin, an outer sphere of general emotion; and the effect of the occurrence of anything in particular was to make the sea submerge the island, the margin flood the text. The great wave now for a moment swept over . . .

The move to Venice is the crucial symbolic step in the novel, the desperate bid for land by which Milly, seeking to avoid her fate, finally ensures it. The land/sea antitheses which the Italian port represents integrate with the action and imagery at this critical juncture to become the literal enactment of the carefully structured image-pattern located in the early sections of the tale. It is precisely at this point that James begins to unfold the vast scaffolding that supports and gives stature to his tragedy: action and imagery coalesce at Venice to a degree of indissolubility. From this powerful conjunction a tensile symbolism derives.

As we have already observed in this study, the abrupt physical actualisation of an initial and extensive verbal imagery, the concretisation of emotion, was a characteristic Jamesian procedure after 1891. In *The Wings of the Dove* and the other late novels it is developed to its furthest limits. In *The Golden Bowl*, for instance, references to cups, containers, bowls and flawed crystals accumulate at moments of crisis, particularly the vending of the Bowl and its destruction, to suffuse the entire novel with symbolic power. In *The Ambassadors*, to take another example, the imagery, once again that of the stream or river of life, is drawn together with the action at the novel's central moment, Strether's accidental encounter with Chad and Madame de Vionnet. Or again, in *The Sacred Fount* the multiple references to clouded vision, gloom and light, accrete at major points to invest the narrator's principal activity, watching and wondering, with something very close to symbolic relevance. And finally, to come back to the novel under discussion, in *The Wings of the Dove* the tension between floating and drowning collects about Milly's sea-girt palace to imbue the geography of her world with a significance and power greater than itself. Venice has become a symbol. Its physical and geographic realities are used by James, in a stroke of inventive genius, to express the literal and imaged facts of Milly's despair.

Without wishing to overstate the point, it should be clear that my implicit argument here is that James's complex technical process, in all the late novels, derives ultimately from Ibsen. With regard to *The Wings of the Dove*, a whole series of Ibsen parallels spring to mind: the sea-imagery and Bernick's shipping firm in *The Pillars of Society*; the water-imagery and the deaths by drowning in *Rosmersholm*; the close interrelation of symbol and action in *The Lady from the Sea*; the streams and the drowned innocents in *The Wild Duck* and *Little Eyolf*. The Ibsen influences on the image/action nexus in *The Wings of the Dove* could have been any or all of these; at this stage in his career, as we have seen, James had fully assimilated Ibsen's method and used it as his own. What we should note is that the symbolic structuring in this novel, and in the others, is essentially without difference (though the degree of application is more intense) from that which James adopted in imitation of Ibsen when he wrote *The Reprobate* more than ten years earlier. The integration of action and image, at a critical turning-point of the plot, had become classically Jamesian.

Soon after his entrance in Book Seventh Lord Mark is given an unusually explicit speech (unusual I mean for James) which points, as directly as a good novelist might dare, to the central symbolism of the tale. James leads up to it carefully. "Do you remember," Lord Mark asks Milly, "something I said to you that day at Matcham—or at least fully meant to?" Milly replies: "Oh, yes. I remember everything at Matcham. It's another life." Lord Mark then makes his explicit statement, a deliberate Jamesian signpost for the wary reader: "Certainly it will be—I mean the kind of thing: what I then wanted to represent for you. Matcham, you know, is symbolic. I think I tried to rub that into you a little.

This is as far as James is prepared to go at this point, but if we turn back a few pages he makes himself quite clear. The portrait episode at Matcham, in which Milly saw her own dead likeness, marked the destruction of all hope. James spells it out in terms of his central image:

> [Milly] had not been so thoroughly alone with him since those moments of his showing her the great portrait at Matcham, the moments that had exactly made the high-water mark of her security, the moments during which her tears themselves, those she had been ashamed of, were the sign of her consciously rounding her protective promontory, quitting the blue gulf of comparative ignorance and reaching her view of the troubled sea.

In the churning waters after Matcham Milly's fragile vessel is wrecked and finally sinks. During her last, great public appearance, the scene in which she wears white and outshines even Kate who "looked her best at night", Milly and her guests at the palace are up to their necks in the encroaching tide. She bears the flood with her:

> [Densher] felt her as diffusing, in wide warm waves, the spell of a general, a kind of beatific mildness. There was a deeper depth of it, doubtless, for some than others; what he, at any rate, in particular knew of it was that he seemed to stand in it up to the neck. He moved about in it, and it made no plash; he floated, he noiselessly swam in it; and they were all together, for that matter, like fishes in a crystal pool.

The point is that Milly's "ark"—so she at one point images her final home—has caved in at the bows. The seas rush in and the vessel founders. Milly's death takes place on a day when the sea itself has become "impossible", and wind and rain lash the windows. James's imagery is consistent to the end.

In exposing the limitations of Bewley's analysis I do not want to suggest that he is wrong to trace the origins of James's Dove in Hawthorne's *The Marble Faun*. What he overlooks, however, is the presence of other important imagery, the manner in which it is developed, and above all the extensive technical differences between the two novels. Bewley sees only that Hilda and Milly live in their turrets above the Italian crowds; what he forgets is that Hilda's tower is her dovecote (and the emblem of Christian spiritual grace in contrast with Donatello's embattlemented worldliness) while Milly's is her burial palace. My point is that Ibsen, who also used the symbolic Dove in *Brand*—a Dove who triumphs in the moment of Death and in the name of Love, proclaiming "He is Deus Caritatis"—taught James how to use the imagery of *The Marble Faun*.

Milly's dove-like qualities are inseparable from her wealth: the two both complement one another and draw strength from their contingency. Her money is a physical part of her, like her hair, like a pair of wings; it is "piled on her back", *the* thing she is.

> . . . it was, all the same, the truth of truths that the girl couldn't get away from her wealth. She might leave her conscientious com-

panion as freely alone with it as possible and never ask a question, scarce even tolerate a reference; but it was in the fine folds of the helplessly expensive little black frock that she drew over the grass as she now strolled vaguely off; it was in the curious and splendid coils of her hair, "done" with no eye whatever to the *mode du jour*, that peeped from under the corresponding indifference of her hat, the merely personal tradition that suggested a sort of noble in-elegance; it lurked between the pages of the uncut but antiquated Tauchnitz volume of which, before going out, she had mechanically possessed herself. She couldn't dress it away, nor walk it away, nor read it away, nor think it away; she could neither smile it away in any dreamy absence nor blow it away in any softened sigh. She couldn't have lost it if she had tried—that was what it was to be really rich. It had to be *the* thing you were.

Even before Milly's first entrance James establishes that important symbolic identification between cash and vast social wings which figures so prominently throughout the rest of the novel. Mrs Lowder, herself a wealthy woman, is imaged as a vulture, an eagle, hovering above the rest and poised on great financial feathers:

> 'You speak", Densher observed, "as if [Aunt Maud] were a vulture."
> "Call it an eagle—with a gilded beak as well, and with wings for great flights . . ."

Later in the novel he reaps this apparently lightly-sown image when transforming, with immense subtlety, and by the most imperceptible of degrees, Milly's bank account into her wings. The process is, as I say, a gradual one, wrought by a touch here, a half-phrase there, or the apparently playful extension of a chance image. During Milly's last public appearance in the novel, for example, the evening when her fortress walls collapse and the flood rushes into the lower chambers, she "sent across towards them [Densher and Kate] in response all the candour of her smile, the lustre of her pearls, the value of her life, the essence of her wealth." Milly simply *is* the priceless pearl she wears about her pretty throat, and by a series of linguistic layers is her money, is her beauty, is her essence. She is what she is; and

> Milly was indeed a dove; this was the figure, though it most applied to her spirit. But he knew in a moment that Kate was just

now, for reasons hidden from him, exceptionally under the impression of that element of wealth in her which was a power, which was a great power, and which was dove-like only so far as one remembered that doves have wings and wondrous flights, have them as well as tender tints and soft sounds.

As Kate gazes across the room in jealous admiration of Milly she succumbs to the power of her presence, of her purse; she vibrates to *the* thing Milly is, her wealth; or, in terms of the novel's dove imagery, she feels the rush of those great wings. Like Hedda, who envies Thea's rich golden hair and yearns to burn it off, Kate wants to rip away Milly's pinions. The fatal error she makes, however, is in assuming that, having torn the wings from the dove, she too will be able to fly. But doves have tender tints and soft sounds as well as wondrous flights. Kate is simply not a dove; she is, in terms of the novel's explicit fauna-imagery, a panther, a beast of prey, who stalks the dove and finally destroys it. Milly's golden wings, as Kate discovers too late, can only be used by herself.

The enormous relief of Milly's death—what we might call a mitigated tragedy—owes its power to her capacity to fly, suddenly, beyond the steadily encroaching tide. By carefully integrating his imagery, then, James brings together in a single startling nexus the Dove, the Flood and the Gold.

> "Our dear dove, then, as Kate calls her, has folded her wonderful wings."
> "Yes—folded them."
> It rather racked him, but he tried to receive it as she intended, and she evidently took his formal assent for self-control. "Unless it's more true", she accordingly added, "that she has spread them the wider."
> He again but formally assented, though strangely enough, the words fitted an image deep in his own consciousness. "Rather, yes—spread them wider."
> "For a flight, I trust, to some happiness greater—"
> "Exactly. Greater."

In this exchange between Merton Densher and Mrs Lowder the three symbols rapidly interchange, establishing new relations which both unite and distinguish. In Aunt Maud's first formal remark Milly's wings are a symbol of her life: as the dove dies she closes her feathers about her. Her next observation, however, develops the image further: the wings are Milly's fortune. Milly's life and Milly's gold conjoin in a single image and then diverge as the text moves on. With her death comes the possibility of an heir. And finally, in a third formulation, Milly's wings bear her spirit aloft to its heavenly reward.

Mrs Lowder's protean metaphor recalls the first occasion on which it was used, when

> it even came to Densher dimly that such wings could in a given case—*had*, in fact, in the case in which he was concerned—spread themselves for protection. Hadn't they, for that matter, lately taken an inordinate reach, and weren't Kate and Mrs Lowder, weren't Susan Shepherd and he, wasn't *he* in particular, nestling under them to a great increase of immediate ease?

Aunt Maud's words "strangely enough . . . fitted an image deep in his own consciousness." It does so not only because of Merton's secret hopes, but also because it is a direct and deliberate reworking of an image already carefully established. The reader, at this moment, becomes Densher.

The manner of James's symbolism at this juncture, as in the earlier, recalls faithfully the Ibsenic process which we have carefully traced in evolution. He might have taken as his technical model almost any of Ibsen's later dramas; he was familiar with them all. *The Wild Duck*, for example, provides in its treatment of the duck-symbol a tempting instance. Hedvig, the wounded little girl, becomes at death a dying bird plunging to the depths of her lake, there to drown. Or *Brand*, again, offers suggestive parallels when Gerd evokes the spiritual Dove which destroys while proclaiming the power of Divine Love. In each case the symbolic transformation of girl to bird suggests possible parallels, although insufficient in my judgment to establish a case for direct influence. As we noted earlier, it is probable that Ibsen's influence had become so general in James's work that specific plays no longer functioned as immediately as before in the evolution of particular fictions.

So far I have tried to illustrate the close and obviously carefully plotted interactions between James's thematic imagery and his concrete symbolism, showing how each operates in a process of mutual reinforcement. It should be clear from this that, unlike Hawthorne, James seldom began with his symbol, but allowed it to emerge more or less organically from the accumulated verbal imagery. Alternatively, knowing beforehand his general symbolic direction, he created in a context of images a slow build-up towards the moment when image and action could coalesce into symbol. His intention, successfully achieved in my view, was to heighten rather than transform the realist effect of his stories. As a young writer his strength had lain in his capacity to combine the vividness of pictorial effect with an acute personal observation, as in, for example, his brilliant portraits in *The Bostonians*: Mrs Farrinder, the militant feminist, who "at almost any time, had the air of being introduced by a few remarks"; or Selah Tarrant, who "looked like the priest of a religion that was passing through the stage of miracles." As he matured, however, he became less satisfied with such general statements and more concerned to "show", in Wayne Booth's celebrated formulation, than to "tell". His commitment to social realism in conjunction with his aesthetic aspirations led him, first, to his melancholy theatrical experience, and then, later, to the more successful attempt to exploit in narrative form the technical expertise he had gained. At about this time he encountered the work of Ibsen, that other great expatriate writer, in which he discovered that it was possible to heighten a realistic effect through the interaction of image and physical fact. This technique he adopted, absorbed, in order to render in his fiction as forcefully as possible thematic ideas, such as the presence of evil in contemporary society, which had been with him almost from the first. His grasp and appreciation of Hawthorne's method, coupled with his admiration for his artistic success, may have encouraged him to follow Ibsen at this point. At all events it is quite clear that in his post-drama fiction we find a discreetly blueprinted structure of images and physical realities which, as in Ibsen, function together with the action to energise what are frequently banal or melodramatic plots.

It has not been my intention in this study to suggest that James ever veered towards plagiarising Ibsen's work. His response to the Norwegian's plays was always creative and, with the possible exception of *The Other House*, never crudely mimetic. Ibsen was a liberating factor in James's artistic evolution, pointing the way to a resolution of the *impasse* of the early eighteen-nineties, and showing him how to resolve many of the technical problems of his later development. Ibsen was the vital link in James's life-long attempt to synthesise the dramatic and the narrative arts.

Select Bibliography

This bibliography is in three sections: A. Studies describing Ibsen's contemporary reception in England and the United States; B. Books and articles which have examined in whole or part the possibility of Ibsen's effect on James's work; C. Accounts of James's involvement with the Victorian theatre.

Clearly there is a degree of overlap between B and C.

A. Ibsen's Contemporary Reception

BURCHARDT, C. B.   *Norwegian Life and Literature* (Oxford University Press, 1920)

DECKER, CLARENCE   *The Victorian Conscience* (Twayne, 1952)

EGAN, MICHAEL   *Henrick Ibsen: The Critical Heritage* (Routledge and Kegan Paul, 1972)

FRANC, MIRIAM   *Ibsen in England* (Four Seas, 1919)

HAUGEN, EINAR   *Ibsen in America* (Norwegian-American Studies and Records, Vol. XX, 1959, pp. 26–43)

B. Henry James and Ibsen

CARGILL, OSCAR   *The Novels of Henry James* (Macmillan, 1961)

EDEL, LEON   *The Other House* by Henry James, edited and introduced by Leon Edel (Rupert Hart-Davis, 1948)

EDWARDS, HERBERT   "Henry James and Ibsen" (*American Literature*, XXIV, May, 1952)

FERGUSSON, FRANCIS   *The Idea of a Theatre* (Anchor Books, 1953)

HOLLAND, LAURENCE   *The Expense of Vision* (Princeton, 1964)

KROOK, DOROTHEA   *The Ordeal of Consciousness in Henry James* (Cambridge University Press, 1967)

ROBINS, ELIZABETH   *Theatre and Friendship: Some Henry James Letters* (London, 1932)

WARREN, AUSTIN   "Myth and Dialectic in the Later Novels" (*Kenyon Review*, V, Autumn, 1943, pp. 551–568)—Reprinted under the title "Symbolic Imagery" in the Twentieth Century Views edition *Henry James*, edited by Leon Edel (Prentice-Hall, 1963)

C.   Henry James and the Theatre

EDEL, LEON   *The Complete Plays of Henry James* (Rupert Hart-Davis, 1949)

— *Guy Domville* by Henry James, a play in three acts with comments by Bernard Shaw, H. G. Wells and Arnold Bennett, edited and introduced by Leon Edel (Rupert Hart-Davis, 1961)

— *Les Années Dramatiques* (Paris, 1931)

— *Henry James: The Middle Years, 1884–1894* (Rupert Hart-Davis, 1963)

LEVY, LEO B.   *Versions of Melodrama: A Study of the Fiction and Drama of Henry James, 1865–1897* (Berkeley, 1957)

WADE, ALAN   *The Scenic Art: Notes on Acting and Drama* by Henry James, edited and with an introduction and notes by Alan Wade (Rupert Hart-Davis, 1949)

WEISENFARTH, JOSEPH   *Henry James and the Dramatic Analogy: A Study of the Major Novels of the Middle Period* (New York, 1963)

Index